CONSULTING SKILLS FOR INFORMATION PROFESSIONALS

Consulting Skills for Information Professionals

Donald M. Arnoudse
L. Paul Ouellette
John D. Whalen

DOW JONES-IRWIN
Homewood, Illinois 60430

*To all the information systems professionals we
have had the privilege to serve as
clients and students*

Acquisitions editor: Susan Glinert Stevens, Ph.D.
Project editor: Mary Lou Murphy-Luif
Production manager: Bette Ittersagen
Jacket design: Mark Swimmer
Compositor: Eastern Graphics
Typeface: 11/13 Times Roman
Printer: Arcata Graphics/Kingsport

Library of Congress Cataloging-in-Publication Data

Arnoudse, Donald M.
    Consulting skills for information professionals.

    Bibliography: p.
    Includes index.
    1. Information resources management.   2. Information
consultants.   I. Ouellette, L. Paul.   II. Whalen,
John D.   III. Title.
T58.64.A76   1989   658.4'038   88–11868
ISBN 1-55623-121-0

Printed in the United States of America

1 2 3 4 5 6 7 8 9 0 K 5 4 3 2 1 0 9 8

PREFACE

One morning in a large insurance company senior management called the information systems department together and laid down a challenge: "What we expect from you is to find ways to use information technology in our company that will transform the insurance business as radically as the automated teller machine networks have transformed banking."

That challenge, and others like it, epitomize the changes that led to the writing of this book. In organization after organization senior management is calling on information systems (IS) to be a key player not just in supporting, but in *transforming* the organization. They are looking for payoff from their information technology investment, not only in increased efficiency and reduced costs, but in new markets, new products, and new ways of doing business. In order to meet that challenge, IS professionals at all levels are taking a hard look at the way they have been doing business, and in many cases are finding that they themselves need to make some fundamental changes—changes in their mission, their skill base, and their methods of working with the users of technology.

This book is for information systems professionals who want to meet that challenge, who want to take positive, practical steps to increase the payoff of their efforts in their organizations. In the ever-growing category of "information systems professionals" we include anyone whose job responsibilities require applying computing and communications technologies to solve an organization's problems and make the most of its opportunities. If you fit that description, the book is addressed to you, whether you are a systems analyst in a Fortune 500 company, a telecommunications manager for a university, a support staffer answering the end-user computing hotline for a government agency, or the person responsible for developing solutions on your department's desktop computer system.

The basic premise of the book is that to meet the challenge, you as an IS professional must work in a *problem-solving partnership* with the users of information technologies. This way of working differs in important ways from how most IS professionals worked in the past. In this relationship, you work in a consultative capacity, with the users of technology as your clients. Redefining this relationship has implications for the kinds of tasks you perform, the kinds of issues you must address, the skills you must develop, and the methods you use.

This book is designed as a practical, "how-to" guide for building problem-solving partnership. Because this way of working involves a different way of thinking about your job and your users, Part 1 begins by building a shared understanding of what problem-solving partnership is all about, how it differs from other ways of working, and what general skills you need to be effective at it. Part 2 then provides a practical framework, which we call the consulting cycle, for working with clients in partnership on all types of IS projects. Part 3 presents some specific partnership techniques and how to use them, and Part 4 outlines ways to be proactive in applying the skills and techniques of partnership in identifying and pursuing high-payoff technology opportunities in your organization.

The ideas in this book are based on the authors' combined experience of more than 50 years in information systems, consulting, and organization development, and specifically on our work with IS professionals from over 700 organizations in developing the skills and techniques that are the heart of the problem-solving partnership approach. The techniques we describe have all been tested and refined "in the trenches" by us and by our clients and students. We as much as anyone know that the challenge facing IS is not an easy one. But we also know that it is the most exciting opportunity, in the history of a field characterized by exciting opportunities, to change the way business does business. We wish you success in meeting this challenge, and hope that this book will help you to achieve it.

ACKNOWLEDGMENTS

It is a pleasure to be able to thank those who, though their names do not appear on the cover, participated directly or indirectly in the development of this book.

Thanks go to associates Karen Rancourt, Nancy Heaton, and Mark Major for their support in developing and refining some of the ideas presented here. Nancy's review of the first-draft manuscript helped push the book to its final form. Thanks also to Dan and Denise Roberts and John Ouellette, too-often-unsung heroes of the office staff. John, in particular, has helped refine some of the material in the book through countless revisions to course workbooks and through preparing articles for trade publications.

Special thanks from Don to Cecil Williams, Kenneth Sole, Edith Seashore, and Jack Sherwood for their contribution to his understanding of the consulting process, and from John to Dr. Joseph M. Ryan and Bruce White, who provided invaluable early feedback on the manuscript based on their experience in internal consulting. Dr. Ryan also made helpful suggestions for the consulting reading list in the Appendix.

Many of the case examples used in the book are based on typical problems brought to us by students in our IS consulting skills workshops, where we test consulting methods and techniques against the realities of their work environment. We thank them for their participation and their enthusiasm for the IS consulting challenge, which constantly renews our own commitment to the field.

And to our wives: from Paul, thanks to Elaine Ouellette, who has been extremely supportive since the book was nothing more than an idea in his head; from Don, deepest appreciation to Colleen Kilcoyne, with whom he continues to discover the essence of true partnership daily; and from John, thanks to Susan O'Keefe, who read the final manuscript with as keen and kind an eye as a spouse could hope for. Without their patience and unstinting support this book would not be.

Donald M. Arnoudse
L. Paul Ouellette
John D. Whalen

CONTENTS

PART 1

WHAT IS PROBLEM-SOLVING PARTNERSHIP?

CHAPTER 1

FROM TECHNICIAN TO PARTNER: THE EVOLUTION OF THE IS PROFESSIONAL

What does it mean to be a problem-solving partner? A number of very practical techniques are involved, and Parts 2 through 4 of this book present these techniques in detail. If you are mainly interested in the how-to of partnership, you might want to start there. But problem-solving partnership also involves what for many information systems (IS) professionals is a new way of looking at their jobs and at the people—most often called "users"—whom they serve. This chapter and the remaining chapters in Part 1 provide a profile of this new IS role—why it is necessary, what kind of skills it requires, what it is like to work this way.

Our first perspective on this new role is an evolutionary one. Problem-solving partnership involves a transformation of the relationship between the IS function and the users of information technology, a major and usually somewhat painful transformation that is going on right now in many organizations. But that transformation is only the latest stage in an ongoing evolution of the role of the IS function, and you, the IS professional.

The information systems function began in most organizations with the introduction of tab equipment in the early 1960s to automate the accounting function. At that time the IS function was usually called EDP, for "electronic data processing." The tab operators, the predecessors of programmers and operators, programmed jobs by plugging different colored wires into boards. Running a job consisted of putting trays and trays of cards through a reader. The IS professional served as a *technician*, operating the machine, rewiring to handle different jobs, running jobs, and clearing jams.

The next era in information technology was ushered in by the IBM 1401, the first major commercial computer. This new equipment was much more sophisticated than the tab equipment which preceded it. The IS function was now usually called DP, or data processing. These were heady days for IS professionals, who were just beginning to see a new and sophisticated career opening up before them. The users at this stage began to be dependent on IS, and the IS professional served as a *chauffeur* to the users. The chauffeur says, "Tell me where you want to go, and I'll take you there. I know how to drive this car, and I'll take you wherever you want to go. But I'll never teach you to drive the car; it's just too complex." Technology was DP's domain, and the users were warned to keep hands off. The user's interface with DP was the little window in the data control area where batches of documents were handed in and reports were picked up once the system had run.

The advent of on-line systems changed the IS function again, and the corresponding name change was to MIS, for "management information systems." The promise of this new name was that managers would be able to manage better given the improved access to information the new systems offered. The introduction of the dumb terminal was the first step in moving part of the organization's technology investment out of the data center and into the hands of the users—a shift in the information infrastructure that continues today.

With on-line systems and the often huge teleprocessing networks that accompanied them, IS professionals gained prestige and power. Their jobs grew in importance as the organization grew to rely on computer systems for survival. This was the era of the IS professional as *high priest*, working in the back room on arcane and complex technologies that the mere mortals who used the terminals could not hope to understand. This is where the idea that IS people are somehow not part of the business got its start. It was reinforced by the seller's market for IS skills during the 70s, when job-hopping for better pay or a more state-of-the-art technical environment was the rule rather than the exception. Secure in the knowledge that they could get another job in a company that would often be in a completely different industry, many IS professionals did not learn much about the business their organization was in. Their "business" was information systems, and their value was in the transferability of that technical skill across industries and organizations.

The users' attitude to IS in this era was often mistrust, based on IS professionals' distance from everyday operations and their inability to talk the users' language without the technical jargon that was so much a part of IS's mystique. But with the terminals in their hands, users at the same time began to understand a little of the technology, to become partners in the information-processing effort. This change created a need for a consulting orientation on the part of IS; however, for the most part, this opportunity was missed.

The late 1970s and the early 1980s saw the introduction of two types of computing tools that further altered the relationship between IS and user. First, software tools that enabled users to do a limited amount of ad hoc inquiries and report writing at their terminals were introduced. With these tools, users became partners with IS in development of report formats and database queries and not just in data entry and access. The development of more powerful fourth-generation languages increased the users' role by enabling them to create and maintain their own databases.

Then the personal computer became a corporate tool. Using new software that truly began to deliver on the claim of ease of use, users began to develop, maintain, and use systems with no involvement by IS. Where IS professionals were involved, as in the formation of the information center, they found that users no longer wanted IS to do the job for them; instead, they wanted support, training, problem resolution, and guidance. In fact, the users were *demanding* services rather than sitting back and taking what IS developed. IS professionals found themselves serving as *coach*—quite a change from the high priesthood of the previous era. The coach teaches the player the techniques but stands in the background when the player goes to bat. Developing user self-sufficiency with the technology rather than keeping users away from it, was the new goal.

This new relationship to the users created quite a bit of conflict with the traditional IS groups, and not simply because they saw their traditional power base being eroded. They also saw the dangers of placing IS technologies in the hands of people who did not understand the disciplines and controls needed to ensure efficiency, integrity, and reliability in the systems they developed. With some justification, they saw end-user computing as creating a chaos of undocumented systems, incompatibilities, duplication of effort, and lack of planning. The users experienced the excitement of having control over their data, as well as the frustration and tedium of the tasks they took over from IS. In the process, they learned more about the technology and its possibilities. In their eagerness to exploit it, they often perceived IS as a roadblock, or at best as uninterested in supporting their efforts.

As we approach the 1990s, IS organizations face a very different environment than the one they faced a decade ago. We can be sure that more and more information systems will be developed and implemented by the user departments. We can also be sure that technological development will continue to outstrip the users' ability to take full advantage of the existing capabilities.

If organizations are to get full benefit from technology's ability to leverage business opportunity, IS and the functional areas must work more closely together. Users need to learn the systems disciplines that will ensure integrity, reliability, and maintainability in the systems they develop. They need to understand current and emerging technologies in order to use them to change the way they do business. And IS needs, in turn, to get closer to the business, closer to the users, to facilitate that learning and to focus its own resources where it can expect the biggest business payoff.

Many IS organizations are taking steps in this direction by "distributing" IS professionals directly into the functional areas, moving them physically closer to the business. Others are training user personnel by the hundreds to be local liaisons with IS and channels for disseminating technology knowledge. For the individual IS professional, working in this environment requires the new relationship with the users that we call *problem-solving partnership*. It is a highly *consultative* relationship, with the IS professional serving as an internal IS consultant, and the user in the role of client. Chapter 2 takes an in-depth look at this new relationship.

CHAPTER 2

STRIKING THE PARTNERSHIP BALANCE: OPTIONS FOR THE IS CONSULTANT/CLIENT RELATIONSHIP

Problem-solving partnership is not just a stage in the evaluation of the IS function—it is an option for you as an individual IS consultant every time you work on a project. In your experience with different kinds of projects, working with clients from different areas and levels in the organization, you have probably found yourself in a number of different work relationships with those clients. Often the relationship you end up with is based on client expectations, the technical characteristics of the project, your own workload, and the skills you bring to the project. The role you assume has a great deal to do with the kind of role the client will take on, both during and after the project: your role will affect, among other things, the client's sense of responsibility for the solution, the level of self-sufficiency with the technology that the client takes away from the project (and correspondingly the amount of postimplementation support and rework you will have to do), and the focus of blame if things go wrong. Understanding your options, and the pros and cons of each one, can help you stay out of roles that are inappropriate and stay alert to the potential problems of each one. Typically, you will find yourself in one of four roles: technical wizard, techical assistant, quiet influencer, or problem-solving partner.

TECHNICAL WIZARD

Bob, an enthusiastic, bright, newly promoted systems analyst in a manufacturing firm, was given his first project leader assignment—to provide a project management system to the engineering department. The organization was highly decentralized, and various engineering groups used their own methods of project management, some manual, some simple scheduling programs written in FORTRAN on the engineering minicomputers, and some personal computer-based systems. Senior management wanted consistency and the ability to summarize project reporting.

Bob accepted the challenge and invested his considerable energies in the analysis. He set up interviews with several engineering managers to determine their requirements. Though they were very busy with the demands of their project-driven environment, they were polite, answered his questions, and gave him the impression that they were supportive of the project, were willing to cooperate in whatever way necessary, and trusted the analyst, who knew the computing environment much better, to come up with the best solution.

Bob summarized the data gathered from his interviews and produced a requirement list that he ran by the engineering managers for approval. Some minor modifications were suggested, but in general his list met with no argument. He then evaluated a number of products on the market that ran on the organization's mainframe computing environment and could support the number of projects underway in the organization. He selected the system that best matched the requirements and got two of the engineering managers to travel to the vendor's site for a demonstration. They agreed that the system produced the kinds of reports that would be needed.

Because senior management supported the goals of the project management system, approval for the purchase was quick and easy, and the system was installed on the mainframe computer. Acceptance tests with test data showed that the system performed as advertised and met the requirements. One engineering manager, known as a good soldier who could be relied on to get things done, was chosen to pilot the system, and began to enter a current project into the system. At this point, word began to circulate that "IS's" scheduling system was inflexible and hard to use. Simon, the administrator assigned to run the system in the pilot group, was particularly vocal and, since he had had no prior exposure to the system, was particularly upset by its limitations. Simon's only other computer experience was with a personal computer spreadsheet, and the relative slowness and lack of flexibility of the mainframe software left him frustrated.

In addition, some project managers sent the word through the grapevine that the system had been set up by IS so that senior management could spy on them at every stage of their projects. The pilot proceeded slower than expected, with major delays over minor steps in the learning curve, and loud complaints from the administrator. When target dates arrived for other project groups to begin using the system, each project manager found reasons to put it off: too critical a project to hazard the delays of learning a new system, lack of terminal equipment, lack of staff to input project data. Months dragged on, and when the senior manager who had initiated the project was transferred, the system quietly died on the vine.

The results? An investment of hundreds of thousands of dollars in software and associated product costs and nearly a man-year of effort in IS and engineering, with no return.

This scenario is an example of the IS consultant in the role of technical wizard. In this scenario, the scales are heavy on the consultant's side. Table 2–1 describes the responsibilities usually taken on by consultant and client in this relationship.

One benefit of this approach is that as consultant in this situation, you have control of the project. This can be a real advantage, especially on short projects where the problem is clearly defined and you have past experience with similar problems. In these situations this role can be a real time-saver. The client may see it this way also. It can be a great relief to drop the project on your desk and forget about it until it is time to review the solution. This role may also be necessary on a high-priority project (say, to meet a government-imposed deadline for new reporting requirements).

However, experience shows that even seemingly short and simple projects can have unexpected twists that make the technical wizard role a risky one. This role has several disadvantages. First, when you take on such a large portion of the responsibility, the client usually does not feel ownership for the project. In our example, the project management system quickly became identified as "IS's system." Lack of client ownership results in all sorts of problems, from lack of cooperation to subtle sabotage. You are much less likely to get full information from a

TABLE 2–1
Responsibilities in the Technical Wizard Relationship

Consultant	Client
• Drives the problem-solving process	• Defines problem, then awaits instructions
• Sees a technical problem, requiring a technical solution	• Sees computer expertise as primary requirement to solve problem
• Collects data, with focus on data relevant to technical system design, installation, and maintenance	• Provides data in response to specific requests
• Takes responsibility for system design and all technical decisions	• Sees solution as the technical wizard's system
• Does not take responsibility for full business implementation of system	• May not take full responsibility for full business implementation either

client who does not feel responsibility for the project. In our example, the engineering managers readily answered the analyst's questions—after all, senior management was known to be behind the project—and overt opposition would have brought attention and pressure down the management chain. However, the engineering managers played an entirely passive role in this process, staying within the framework of the analyst's questions and volunteering no information or participation. The analyst saw this acquiescence as agreement and assumed that the lack of enthusiasm was simply part of the "engineering mentality."

A second disadvantage is that you are more likely to "force-fit" a technology solution that does not meet the real needs of the client. In our example, the IS analyst's lead role led him to assume that the system would reside on IS's mainframe, a system with which the engineering managers had no familiarity. With more involvement on the part of the engineering group in the design, the option of installing the package on the engineering minicomputers might have surfaced as a way to reduce resistance and promote engineering ownership of the solution. Senior management's requirements for summary reporting could then be handled by loading summary data up to the mainframe for consolidation. As was true in our case, when a technical wizard's project fails, the blame is all too readily laid at IS's door.

A third problem with this role is that even if the project is a smashing success, the client is not educated in the process. Little has been done to improve his or her self-sufficiency with IS technology—a critical goal in today's environment where more and more computing must be done by end-users. Equally important, he or she has not been educated in the process of partnership, in using IS effectively as a consulting resource while building his or her own function's IS expertise. The next time this client has a problem, you will have to begin again from square one. And you have also fostered an expectation that you will solve the client's problems with little participation on the client's part.

This leads to the fourth disadvantage, this role is an overload-builder. In today's environment, where the IS resource is being spread thinner and thinner, this role can be a real danger if used too often. It widens the gap between IS and the business rather than forging partnership to bridge that gap.

TECHNICAL ASSISTANT

Donna, a security manager for a small government contractor, went to the organization's IS manager to get help with a database project. She wanted to track employee security clearances and maintain a history for each employee, including when particular levels of clearance were granted, when clearances were revoked, and any security problems connected with that employee. Donna had a sharp young administrator, Glen, on her staff who had taken extensive training on the fourth-generation language supported by the IS group. Glen had also successfully developed some simple databases and reports for the department, helping them to track security incidents and to keep better tabs on parking permits for company lots. In this case, however, Glen had developed a detailed specification for the new system but had been pulled off the project to direct preparations for an upcoming government security audit. Donna wanted the new system operational in two months so that it could be demonstrated to the government auditors. Would the IS group help out in this pinch to support the organization's goal of a good security rating?

The IS manager, eager to be perceived as a team player and support a highly visible organizational goal (this was the period of the Walker spy trials), looked over the specification worked up by the security analyst. It was detailed and thorough, and the system itself did not appear complex. Checking his project log, he noted that Tim, a junior programmer/analyst with experience in the fourth-generation language, was available. The two managers agreed that Tim would turn the specification into a working system in time for the audit.

Tim met with Glen to review the specification and spent three weeks developing the database and report formats. He then obtained some sample data from the security department, entered it, and prepared a demonstration for Glen, who was pleased with the system. Two weeks before the audit, Glen asked if Tim could assist in loading a list of employees and some basic personnel data from the human resources database into the clearance system to avoid retyping that information from written reports. When Tim went to the personnel administrator (who was the custodian of the human resource system) to arrange the transfer, she flew into a rage, chased Tim out of the room, and told him that the data was not to be provided to anyone except through reports approved by her group. The personnel director got wind of the project and mentioned it to the corporate internal auditor, who immediately turned white at the prospect of government auditors seeing multiple and inconsistent databases containing sensitive personnel data. He called the IS manager to ask why he was involved in such unproductive and poorly controlled projects.

It later became clear that Donna and the personnel administrator had had several unpleasant encounters over previous personnel issues. This political issue lay waiting to trip up a project that was viewed as a straightforward technical exercise. The end result? For the client, who had a legitimate need to track security clearances more closely, no solution. For the programmer/analyst, a month of wasted effort. For IS, a painful drop on the credibility scale with three client groups.

This scenario may be extreme, but the results are not untypical of projects where IS takes what we call the "technical assistant" role. This role has become more common as clients become more sophisticated in the use of IS technology. In this situation, the scales are weighted more heavily on the client side, and you become a temporary staff person for the client. The client has analyzed the problem, selected the approach to solve it, and wants you to follow orders and implement his or her solution. The responsibilities in this situation are summarized in Table 2–2.

TABLE 2–2
Responsibilities in the Technical Assistant Relationship

Consultant	Client
• Accepts client's problem analysis and solution	• Drives the problem-solving process
• Does technical design and installation according to client preferences	• Specifies the solution as well as the problem
• Awaits further instructions	• Awaits prescribed solution

There are instances where this role is appropriate or necessary. For example, it may make sense to play this role if you have worked with the client in the past and have a high level of confidence in the client's expertise in the area under consideration. In many organizations, users have acquired considerable expertise with development tools such as fourth-generation languages and personal computer software. Providing added technical manpower on a high-priority project for such a client can be a real relationship builder; it can also turn this expert client into a valuable resource for the IS consultant on future projects. You may also decide to take this role if the project presents a foot-in-the-door opportunity with a highly desirable client. In these cases, you may make the conscious decision to take the risks inherent in this approach.

And there are risks. Most IS professionals feel uncomfortable with this role because of its transfer of control to the client. Ironically, though the client has assumed control of the solution, responsibility for project failure will most likely still be laid at your door. Protests that you had no real role in devising the solution, that you were just following orders, will gain little sympathy. After all, you should know better. It is your job to ensure that solutions are appropriate and sound. Equally ironic is the tendency of the technical assistant role to build overload just as quickly as the technical wizard role. Being at the beck and call of a single client may be manageable, but being in that position with 10 is a nightmare. And with demands on IS resources only increasing, it will probably be the exceptional project where this approach is justified.

In addition to soaking up your time on the current project, the technical assistant role does not use your expertise in defining problems and identifying solution options. And it runs the risk of building a reputation for this type of assistance that may be hard to reverse. One of the goals of today's IS organization is to leverage its scarce talent by having IS professionals used as higher-level resources. The technical assistant role, if used inappropriately, works directly against that goal.

Our warnings about the dangers of these two roles do not mean that we think they should be eliminated. Both you and the client should be aware of the risks involved. If the goal is to build a reputation for partnership and to forge closer ties to the business, then IS should aim to reduce their work as technical wizard and technical assistant to 10 to 20 percent of their effort.

QUIET INFLUENCER

Jim, a marketing manager, was working with an IS team to revamp the office automation strategy for the marketing department. One day he stopped by to see Claire, an IS analyst he had worked with successfully on a marketing database project. Claire was not involved with the office automation project. After some small talk, Jim began asking Claire questions about office automation technologies and how to implement them. He told Claire he was just getting some background for the project he was involved in so that he could understand the whole issue of office automation better. Claire, enjoying the role of authority on technology matters, gave Jim her views and some examples of office automation implementation she had seen in the past. Jim asked such questions as: "Does it make sense to implement an OA system just to get electronic mail capability?" "Should you pilot an OA system first to work the bugs out before full implementation?" "Does it work to put terminals on manager's desks to get them to use electronic mail?"

They talked for 20 minutes and Jim thanked her for her time. Three days later, Claire was called in to her boss's office, where Lee and Sarah, the leaders of the marketing office automation project, were waiting with fire in their eyes. They wanted to know why Claire was second guessing their OA plans with their client and undermining their credibility. They went on to recount the morning's meeting with Jim, at which he had demanded that the team change its plan to conform to his strategy, which he had "verified with Claire," who "had done such a good job on the database project and knew his department much better than they did."

Claire responded that she had not tried to undermine their plan, and that she had only discussed OA in general terms with Jim. She did not even know that they had a plan in place. In fact, Jim's framing of the questions led her to believe that there was no plan in place!

Claire had been placed in the role of quiet influencer. This role can be a powerful one, but in Claire's case, it turned into a disaster—in part because she was not aware of the role she was playing. The responsibilities in the quiet influencer scenario are listed in Table 2–3.

This role is a potentially powerful one for the internal IS consultant. Being effective in this role requires a high level of credibility in the organization, usually based on a solid track record of successes and a reputation for handling political and other organizational issues effectively with professional tact and sensitivity. Without this reputation, you probably won't be asked to play this role very often, and if you attempt to play it proactively, your attempts at influence will probably have little impact.

There are some real advantages to working in this role. It enables you to play a significant part in project efforts with minimal time investment. It puts you in a position to work at a level of openness with clients that may not be achievable when working in other roles. And it builds a strong influence network in the organization, giving you more

TABLE 2–3
Responsibilities in the Quiet Influencer Relationship

Consultant	Client
• Is typically removed from direct involvement in the problem-solving process	• Goes to consultant for objective perspective on project/problem
• Acts as a sounding board, helps defuse client emotions	• Shares issues, concerns with consultant
• Influence depends on credibility with client and rest of organization	• Sees consultant as leader, authority, or trustworthy source of information
• Has great potential to shape events in problem-solving process	• May modify problem-solving approach or own attitudes based on consultant's perspective
• May use influence with other parties to support problem-solving effort	

insight into how the organization operates as well as more leverage in what goes on.

There are some potential dangers in this role, as well. Since you are not directly involved, your influence may not "stick," and events may take a different course. This role is like giving advice to a friend—even though the friend seems to receive it positively, it may have no impact on the friend's behavior. Your indirect involvement can be a problem for your own credibility if handled improperly. You can lose the trust of your IS colleagues if they see you undermining or second-guessing their efforts; you can lose credibility if the problem-solving effort fails, even if the reasons for failure were outside your influence; and if the effort is successful, your personal recognition for that success will be limited.

This role requires more consulting skill than the technical wizard or technical assistant roles. If you play the quiet influencer and do not see all the issues involved in the situation, your influence can actually be harmful. You are usually asked to comment or offer advice on a situation based on the snapshot of that situation provided by the client. Your ability to round out the picture using probing questions and to read between the lines is vital to avoiding the dangers of this role. Since your first reaction to being approached by a client may be to feel flattered, it is important to keep an eye on those dangers. As Claire found in our example, those dangers include being used by a client as an "expert witness" to confirm what the client already thinks he or she knows. In this situation, the client may frame the issues to support his or her position, hoping to get an endorsement from you that can be used as leverage elsewhere. You can attempt to preempt this by carefully framing your comments and qualifying your advice, but you have little control over what the client does with your suggestions outside the meeting room. Therefore, you should be careful to validate what the client brings to you and touch base with others involved in the project to ensure that your comments are not misinterpreted or misused.

PROBLEM–SOLVING PARTNER

Susan was a project leader running a systems development project for a manufacturing system. Her client was Carl, a manufacturing manager. Phase 1 had been completed, and the project leader had to present the team's recommendations to the senior management information systems steering committee to get approval to proceed. Susan set up a meeting with Carl to develop a strategy for the upcoming review. Her suggested agenda was to pool their knowledge about the members of the steering committee in order to understand the audience. She especially wanted to understand the committee's relationships with and attitudes toward Carl's department. Susan told Carl that she would bring along another IS manager who had gone before the board a few weeks earlier and run into some problems. Carl agreed, and suggested that before their meeting he would pay a visit to a fellow manufacturing manager who had worked with one member of the steering committee on past projects.

At the meeting they brainstormed a profile of the committee to ensure that their presentation would push the right business "hot buttons" and avoid the committee's "stop buttons." Their profile included the fact that the two members of the committee with the most manufacturing knowledge were also on a senior management task force for quality improvement. Susan and Carl put together an outline for a presentation that would make the project's impact on manufacturing quality explicit.

Their discussion with the other IS project leader revealed that his problems had resulted from an impression at the review meeting that the client on the project was not fully up on the project. Though the client was firmly behind the project, this lack of awareness about project issues was seen as a sign of low priority, and the project had been postponed indefinitely. Susan suggested that they avoid this problem by sharing the presentation duties in the review meeting, with Carl taking the lead. Carl agreed.

Carl's talk with his fellow manager proved a valuable source of profile information but also had another benefit. The manager was impressed enough with the project that she agreed to voice her support to the steering committee member from manufacturing at her upcoming monthly meeting with him.

Carl and Susan prepared a list of key points from their presentation in advance and circulated it to the steering committee members for review. They checked with each one several days before the meeting to address any questions.

Their profile revealed that one of the members of the steering committee, Sam Mancini, was rumored to be strongly opposed to the project. Susan's track record included a successful project in Sam's department, and she had some credibility with his group. Susan polled her network of contacts to get some idea of Sam's concerns and found that he was involved in a similar project in another division of the company where the result had been an expensive failure. Susan made two phone calls to get the details on that project from contacts in that division and arranged a one-on-one meeting with Sam. During the meeting she summarized the concerns she had heard and asked if they were accurate. Sam agreed that they were. She then asked for a chance to address those concerns and did so in a 10-minute briefing. When she left she had reduced Sam's list of concerns and impressed him with the thoroughness of her attention to the potential problems.

On the day of the meeting, Carl and Susan went to the steering committee meeting early, chatted with the committee members, listened to the preceding presentations to see what kinds of issues were being raised, and used that information to focus the presentation on the spot. The project was approved.

Susan's approach to this piece of the project effort is an example of the problem-solving partnership relationship. The consultant/client scales are more or less evenly balanced; neither partner takes on a disproportionate share of responsibility, and both are fully involved in the project. As you can see, this approach also involves both consultant and client working the human or organizational side of the project as hard as the technical side. The responsibilities in this relationship are summarized in Table 2–4.

In balancing the scales, a surprising thing happens. The process becomes highly interactive. Communication between you and the client becomes a much more important part of the process. Control is negotiated, point by point, as the project proceeds. And this negotiation leads to a sense of joint ownership, a sense that the plan laid out is "our" solution. In this relationship, accountability for success or failure is shared, because the joint belief in the project and enthusiasm for the selected solution are carefully developed and maintained.

Another surprising thing happens when you work in this relationship. Your expertise and leadership broaden to include not only the technical area but the problem-solving process. Responsibility for technical aspects of the project are now negotiated just like the other aspects. This change in the IS professional's role is at the heart of the problem-solving partnership approach.

In addition to the sense of joint ownership and responsibility, this relationship typically has the following benefits:

TABLE 2–4
Responsibilities in the Problem-Solving Partner Relationship

Consultant	*Client*
• Serves as change agent • Has expertise in technology and in the problem-solving process and provides the framework for this process	• Serves as change manager • Has expertise in the business functions and has decision-making accountability

- Both drive the problem-solving process
- Roles are negotiated
- Two-way communication is designed into the project
- The focus is on the business problem and the work relationship in addition to the technical problem
- Both have critical pieces of the puzzle
- Action plan is designed jointly
- Both actively identify needed data and jointly analyze the implications
- Both teach and learn from the other

- A problem-solving relationship is developed that will be the basis for success on future projects and will add to your network of resources and information sources in the organization.
- You and the client gain a better understanding of each other's functions.
- The client is educated in the process of solving problems with technology.
- Over the long term, overload, including support of systems developed, will be reduced.
- You become a higher-level resource and are able to serve more clients.

For the IS department drowning in user requests and at the same time fighting to manage end-user computing activity, this approach is the single most effective tool we have found. Applied correctly, it will move the user base along the technology learning curve while changing the IS function's role from a purely operational or tactical one to a strategic one. At the same time, the problem-solving partner role improves the IS consultant's knowledge of and influence in the functional areas so that future initiatives go more smoothly.

There are some disadvantages to this role. The most obvious is that it requires much more time up front for the client and, in many cases, for you. Thus, getting clients to work this way will require some education and marketing. To a client who is used to using you as a technical wizard, for example, your request to work in partnership will seem like an attempt to get the client to do your job. IS groups across the country face this dilemma with technology users who have been ably trained by IS to drop their problems on the IS professional's lap for technical attention.

PROFILE OF THE PROBLEM-SOLVING PARTNER

What makes the problem-solving partner role different is not primarily what the IS consultant does, but how he or she does it. The consultative approach underlying this role requires a different way of thinking, a different conception of the job of working with information technology. This whole book is designed to flesh out this new way of thinking, but to begin the process we have developed a list of 15 key characteristics of how a problem-solving partner works:

1. Working with clients in an equal partnership. When a consultant takes on a client, the client's goals become his or her goals, and the consultant and client take on equal responsibility for the success of the solution. It becomes "our" project. Without this fundamental buy in by both the client and the consultant, there is no basis for a partnership relationship.

2. Seeing things from the client's perspective. It is difficult (if not impossible) for a consultant to support a client if he or she cannot first see the problem at hand from the client's point of view, understanding what the client thinks and feels about it and why.

3. Focusing on the work relationship with the client as well as the technical problem at hand. The problem-solving partner pays careful attention to the human side of the consulting effort because the best technical solution can fail if the work relationship creates an atmosphere of mistrust or frustration.

4. Communicating in the client's own language. The effective IS consultant avoids technical jargon of all sorts and presents information in terms the client understands.

5. Working to build client trust, confidence, and commitment. The quality of the information the client provides, the cooperation he or she gives, the resources he or she makes available to the consultant—in short, the markings of a successful project—are all directly proportional to the trust the client has in the consultant and the commitment and confidence he or she has for the project effort.

6. Absorbing information and redefining it as solvable problems. The consultant's job is problem definition and clarification. But this is not limited to knowing what technology to apply to a problem. It includes helping the client understand the problem better, slicing huge problems into manageable pieces, and building client enthusiasm and commitment to solving them.

7. Keeping the focus on desired results. The consultant is responsible, in any dealings with a client, for keeping the problem-solving effort on track. That includes identifying and dealing with client resistance, changing finger-pointing into neutral problem statements, getting beyond negative generalizations, acting as facilitator in meetings to structure and guide the discussion according to the project agenda.

8. Generating and presenting options for solution. As clients become more sophisticated in their use of information technology, defining options becomes a larger part of IS's role. In many cases the client will have responsibility for developing and implementing the option selected. In any case, putting the responsibility for choosing an option in the client's hands is essential to building commitment to the solution.

9. Mobilizing effective action once a problem is defined. The effective IS consultant *makes things happen* and is successful at identifying and mobilizing the necessary resources to put plans into action. He or she builds and manages a resource network both within and outside the organization to get things done.

10. Working with (not around) tension and conflict. The successful IS consultant knows that tension and conflict are natural whenever the change involved in the project is significant. The good consultant learns to deal creatively with conflict and does not avoid it or get involved in counterproductive political or personal battles.

11. Being concerned and committed without taking anything personally. The consultant needs a bit of a thick hide, because there will be plenty of opportunities to feel personally affronted by clients or other parties. To be effective, the consultant must master the art of being wholeheartedly involved in a project and committed to its success without taking problems, resistance, roadblocks, or conflict personally.

12. Minimizing long-term client dependence on IS. A key long-range goal of problem-solving partnership is to make clients self-sufficient in the use of technology, not to prolong their dependence on IS. Building self-sufficiency does not put IS out of business; it makes IS a higher-level resource, able to focus more energy on strategic directions and less on hand-holding.

13. Facilitating (not taking over) the client's job responsibilities. Sticking close to the role of facilitator in client relationships is a key to establishing the consulting model. Making the client's goals the consultant's goals does not mean doing his or her job.

14. Staying out of no-win situations. It is the consultant's responsibility to read the dynamics of project-related situations, to be on the lookout for dead ends that will do nothing but sap resources, and to be able to avoid such projects without losing credibility with clients.

15. "Loading the deck" for success by preselling and building commitment wherever necessary. The consultant is responsible for scouting out the political and organizational aspects of a project and working them proactively. This means getting the right people's support early, identifying and minimizing potential roadblocks, and building and maintaining a solid consensus in favor of the course the project is taking.

The role of problem-solving partner as described here poses a major problem—it requires a broader set of skills than those of the other roles you may play. The next chapter describes the necessary skills and presents some methods for strengthening them.

CHAPTER 3

FOUR SETS OF SKILLS FOR PROBLEM-SOLVING PARTNERS

Given the demands of the problem-solving partnership, what makes someone good at it? Certain personality traits—like patience, energy, empathy, being a self-starter, having an interest in communicating with people—are very helpful in candidates for IS consulting assignments, because they are very hard to learn. But as with musical talent, not being born a prodigy doesn't mean you can't learn to play. In fact, we have identified four sets of skills that make for effective IS consulting, and all of these can be developed and improved through initiative, training, and experience:

- Technical skills.
- Human interaction skills.
- Business context skills.
- Consulting framework skills.

You are probably stronger in some areas than others, but an effective training plan for IS consulting should cover all four of these areas. The following sections describe each set of skills along with strategies for strengthening them.

TECHNICAL SKILLS

Of course, technical skills are critical for your success as an IS consultant. No amount of skill in the people or business sides of consulting can make up for a lack of expertise in the effective use of information technologies. If you are like most IS professionals, this is your area of greatest strength, where your education, training, and experience have been focused. You need to maintain and develop these technical skills to keep pace with technological change.

In today's business environment, with more and more computing being done by users within their own functional areas, IS will increasingly be called on to clarify problems and identify solution options, with the client responsible for selecting and implementing the best solution. To serve effectively in this role, you must have a working knowledge of a broad range of technologies, rather than, or in addition to, a single specialty. Regular cross-training can ensure that the IS group is not composed of small groups of experts in each particular technology. Cross-training should be an integral part of the IS training schedule and can often be accomplished using staff experts as trainers. This has the added benefit of building relationships among staff members.

Cross-training ensures that the IS group will not be caught short if one staff member leaves the company or goes on vacation when a key client needs a particular skill. It spreads the skills more evenly, providing management with more flexibility in project assignments. It also helps avoid stagnation and apathy among staff members who have been working with the same set of tools for years. Most important, it makes staff members less likely to apply an improper technology to a problem simply because it is the only one they are familiar with. What if such cross-training is not offered in your IS organization? Take it one step at a time—identify where your skills need to be broadened in this area, find a staffer with the knowledge to train you (preferably one who can benefit by an exchange of skills with you), and market to your supervisor the benefits of building this training into your schedule. (Most supervisors will try such an exercise as an experiment if they see potential value to the group.) Then go after the next area, and soon you will have the basis for lobbying for a full-blown departmental cross-training program.

HUMAN INTERACTION SKILLS

The problem-solving partner role involves you in a highly interactive problem-solving process. Skill in communicating with the client is vital to the development of a solid partner relationship. You need solid skills in the following areas of human interaction in order to be effective.

Communication Skills

This category includes the ability to get a point across to others with clarity and precision. The effective IS consultant must be a good listener. He or she must be able to foster enthusiasm, support, and confidence through communication with others, including clients, staff, superiors, and management. In short, the consultant must be aware of and in control of communications with others and use communication skills as tools to build consulting success.

Three specific kinds of communication skills are particularly important: presentation, interviewing, and negotiation skills. Presentation skills are needed for the wide variety of formal and informal presentations that the typical IS consultant must give. Whether outlining solution options and recommendations to a client, explaining the IS function to a new vice president, or motivating your staff for a difficult project, you must always be ready to make the most of an opportunity to present. (Some methods for preparing IS presentations and specific presentation opportunities are discussed in Part 4.) In order to make the most of these opportunities, you must be comfortable and poised in front of people and able to target your presentation to the audience.

Because the problem-solving partnership relationship is highly interactive, interviewing and negotiation skills are necessary elements in successful consulting. The ability to use meetings and interviews to build client confidence, motivation, and commitment as well as obtain quality data is one of your best assets. This book provides proven techniques for improving these skills.

Well-developed written communication skills are also necessary. On any given day you may need to craft a concise, on-target memo that cements a client relationship and builds trust, or write a newsletter article about important technology issues in language that clarifies, educates, and motivates nontechnical staff.

Influence Skills

IS consulting is an influence job par excellence. It often involves a task force or project environment where formal authority is not the basis for getting things done. You must be able to establish and maintain a broad range of supportive relationships across functional and hierarchical lines. You have as much opportunity as anyone in the organization—including the CEO—to work with all the functional areas of the organization and all the hierarchical levels. To manage this broad client base effectively, supportive contacts throughout the company are vital.

These contacts can include clients, supportive managers, experts in key areas, information sources, administrative people who can grease the right wheel to speed up part of a project, and the building maintenance people who can make sure that the projector is in place and working for that important presentation. They can be outside the company, including vendors, counterparts in other organizations, external consultants, industry experts, anyone who helps you do your job more effectively. These people are resources just as important—if not more so—than your staff or management. This network of relationships is maintained through regular, deliberate contact with these people that provides them with return value whenever possible.

You must also be able to handle accountability without authority. The mark of an influence-oriented job is just this—being responsible for getting things done without formal authority over those whose support and assistance are required to do so. Marshalling resources that report outside your area can be intimidating; it requires careful attention to building coalitions, making sure all the right people are informed and "on board" to make a project work, minimizing resistance wherever possible, and maintaining commitment and momentum.

BUSINESS CONTEXT SKILLS

It would be hard to find an IS manager who would not agree that knowledge of the business environment is critical for today's IS professional. Yet until very recently little concrete action was taken to build this kind of expertise in the IS staff. Take the following self-assessment quiz about your business context knowledge:

1. What is your organization's charter or mission?
2. Name three key objectives from this year's business plan.
3. Describe how one of the projects you are working on ties into those objectives?
4. How much profit (if you work in a for-profit business) did the organization make on how much revenue last year?
5. How do those numbers compare to the results of the previous year?
6. Which functional areas are the current hot areas, key to the business's success?

7. Which are the key problem areas?
8. Who (if you are in a competitive organization) are your organization's three most important competitors?
9. How does the organization stand in market share compared to those other companies?
10. What are three important innovations in your industry over the past five years?

It is just about impossible to build an IS function that really contributes to organizational success if IS consultants do not know the answers to these kinds of questions and more. Of course, this is not only true of IS; everyone in the organization who expects to make an impact should be in touch with the business context. Unfortunately, IS was long viewed as a technical function that did not need such knowledge, and the sellers market for skilled IS professionals, which encourages job-hopping to boost salaries, has done little to foster interest in learning the business.

The best skill-builder in this regard is actual experience in the business (outside IS). For this reason it is becoming more common for IS managers to recruit for the IS function among the other functional areas. However, even if your first position in the organization is in IS, there are a number of ways to build your knowledge of the business. One of the simplest and most effective is regular contact with past, current, and potential clients in order to stay in touch with their needs and concerns. Contact with clients at lunch, in after-work activities, in simply walking around and touching base, is moving IS out of the back room in a basic, simple, but very real sense. And the organization will respond. The first reaction may be surprise, but in the long run the result will be a different image for IS.

One of the simplest ways to stay in touch with the issues driving your business is to read what your clients read. Most IS professionals read computer industry magazines to maintain their technical expertise. It is equally important to read the industry magazines that focus on the business your organization is in. To prevent this from becoming a burden, your group can agree to assign each person in the department a particular industry publication. That person's duty is to read the publication regularly and identify articles of special interest to the group. Then have a support person assemble and circulate copies of these articles to the entire group. A similar method that requires more time during business hours but encourages discussion of business issues is to hold a monthly reading report meeting and have each person summarize key issues picked up from the publications he or she is responsible for.

A similar strategy can be used for seminars and conferences. In addition to attending events focusing on IS technologies, attend industry events on the business side. Many industries have associations that sponsor meetings and conferences; this is where clients stay in touch with hot issues and trends. This information is invaluable for understanding the broader competitive context of the specific problems clients bring to IS, and for being able to talk their language on these issues.

A good long-term career development strategy is to plan an education program on the business. This may include industry seminars, in-house courses, exposure to different areas of the business, courses at a local business or technical university, and a list of readings. More IS organizations are building such programs into their regular IS training curriculum, an effort which requires assessing needs, building support among IS management and supervisors, and constructing a program that has a tangible payoff. If this kind of training program does not exist in your organization, you can influence events in that direction by making yourself a pilot. Sell your supervisor on the value of testing the idea, and commit to spreading what you learn around the group, and to reporting back on what works and what doesn't work in building your business context knowledge.

A strategy we call business exposure is often part of such an education program. Human resources professionals have long used a method called career exposure, in which a person works in a particular department for a period of 30 to 90 days in order to determine whether he or she is interested in pursuing a career in that area. In business exposure, the goal is not to evaluate a potential career, but to learn about a particular functional area within the organization. On a regular schedule, IS professionals are sent to observe and learn in one of the functional areas: marketing, engineering, accounting, financial planning, warehousing, production control, and so on. The schedule for a single functional area might be one-half day per week for four weeks. The person who goes out to the areas is not there to solve problems or to work on IS projects, but to observe, unobtrusively, what the department does. What is their workday like? What are their major concerns and headaches? How do they approach problems? Who are the major players in the organization? Who are the technology experts or supporters?

The ground rules for business exposure must be clearly defined and the purpose of the strategy explained to the functional managers and their staff. And of course prior management approval must be obtained. But if handled correctly this method builds valuable understanding of the business into the IS staff. It can also establish a relationship between IS and the department that did not exist before, and that relationship itself can be a channel for valuable information about the department and how IS can serve it better. The next time someone from that department comes to IS with a problem, the time spent in observation will likely be regained in a reduction of the time required to get the "lay of the land" in that department.

CONSULTING FRAMEWORK SKILLS

A fourth type of skill needed by the IS consultant is a framework that systematizes the consulting side of IS projects the way that structured methodologies systematize the technical side. For most IS professionals, working these issues does not come naturally; they need a structure—a set of processes and procedures—to help build a consulting discipline. Such a framework also helps to build consistency across the IS group in working with clients. This consistency in turn builds client confidence and, as a large base of clients are exposed to the framework, reduces project delays and resistance because the clients are familiar with the consulting process. Because such a framework is central to building problem-solving partnership, we have devoted Part 2 to a detailed description of a framework we call the consulting cycle.

PART 2

A FRAMEWORK FOR PARTNERSHIP: THE CONSULTING CYCLE

CHAPTER 4

THE CONSULTING CYCLE: AN OVERVIEW

Most IS organizations use some type of system development life cycle (SDLC), marking out the stages of a development project. Many use a structured programming method that sets standards for the actual coding of applications programs to make them easier to maintain and enhance. In IS groups where substantial resources are focused on major application development projects, structured methodologies may also be applied to the analysis and design stages of the development life cycle.

These tools are all valuable; they build discipline and quality control into the development process. We will outline in this chapter a tool—the consulting cycle—that is designed to do the same for the consultative side of IS projects—the organizational issues, the human issues, the political issues that so often make or break them. The stages of the consulting cycle, and the tools and techniques described in each stage, are designed to help you work effectively as a problem-solving partner. They will help you see that these issues are neither beyond your control nor outside your responsibilities, and to help you to be proactive—and successful—in working on them.

STAGES OF THE CYCLE

The consulting cycle looks at the project from the point of view of the work relationship between IS and the user/client and focuses on fostering a solid, productive consulting relationship. IS professionals in end-user computing support have found the cycle particularly helpful because the traditional development methodologies are so often too complex for their short-turnaround projects with heavy user involvement. When used in a large-project environment, the consulting cycle raises awareness of the "human side" issues and gives project team members concrete, practical ways to handle them in the course of typical project activities such as data collection.

The consulting cycle (see Figure 4–1) consists of nine stages:

1. Initial Contact. This phase is the first impression, the first meeting between you and your prospective client. In a small-scale project it may be 20 minutes long. But that 20-minute meeting is so important that we identify it as a separate stage to ensure that you make the most of it.

2. Contracting. This is the clarification of goals, roles, and relationships that defines your working relationship with the client on a project. For a long-term project a signed and reviewed service request document may result. A short project may only require a sense of comfort and clarity about who is doing what and by when. In all cases, this stage demands solid communications skills to ensure that the project starts out on the right track and stays there.

3. Data Collection and Analysis. This phase is familiar to systems analysts: it focuses on how to get the information needed to understand the business problem and work toward an effective solution. The consulting cycle methodology looks at these tasks from the perspective of the partnership relationship with the client and provides some detailed techniques for building client trust, confidence, and motivation.

4. Recommendations. A basic premise of the consulting cycle is that your job is to clarify solution alternatives and present them to the client. These solutions may involve selection of technologies, development methods, and staffing and other resources. All your skills are needed to ensure that the client understands the implications of the options presented and can make a decision with confidence.

5. Decision Making. Once recommendations are laid out, the client makes a decision to support one, or not to support any, or to negotiate a modified recommendation, or to propose a new one. Whatever the case, this is the client's stage; your job is to clarify options and expected results.

6. Development, Assistance, and Training. In large-scale development projects where IS is designing and coding an application, this phase would incorporate the detailed design and programming. In projects where the client is taking on the development task, this stage

FIGURE 4–1
The Consulting Cycle

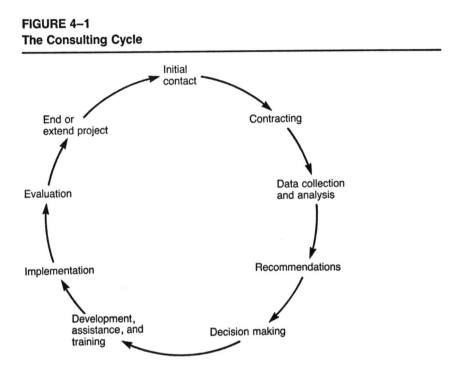

consists of appropriate assistance from IS and any training needed by the user to perform that task.

7. Implementation. This phase covers the steps required to put the system into place in the organization, including installation, test periods, further user training, and other assistance where necessary.

8. Evaluation. This phase tests for success. How does the solution test out in reality? Evaluation methods will vary—the important thing is to build evaluation into the cycle.

9. End or Extend Project. As the diagram indicates, the consulting cycle really is a cycle. It acknowledges that the reality of IS projects rarely follows a straight line. Business being what it is, we are likely to get to the end to find that we have more work to do. In many cases, doing the project itself clarifies the original problem, or identifies new ones. With traditional methodologies this is often seen as a failure: "If only we had gotten that spec right the first time," "If only the users would make up their minds." In reality, however, these new (or clarified) problems are often the natural result of the changing, fuzzy world

FIGURE 4–2
Consulting Cycle Integrated with System Development Life Cycle

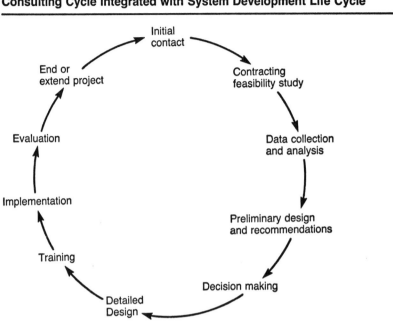

we work in. So rather than building failure into our methodology by aiming for an "end" where we have solved the problem once and for all, we have an "end or extend" phase where we recognize and allow for the decision to continue, in which case we identify any further work as an extension and begin the cycle again.

As we have stressed, this cycle can be applied to any type of IS project, from a request to evaluate packaged software for a personal computer user to a large-scale system development project. It can be adapted and integrated with any other development methodology. For example, the cycle has been adapted for large development projects by combining it with the traditional systems development life cycle. (See Figure 4–2.)

CHAPTER 5

STAGE 1: INITIAL CONTACT

Picture your first meeting with a new client. The client, who has a business need, looks to you for help with that need. You arrive at the client's door. Both you and the client have something at risk, both have anxieties about how things will go; both are evaluating each other, testing the waters. The client is wondering if she can trust you, if you are competent, if the two of you can work together, if this is going to take longer than expected and disrupt her next meeting. You have similar concerns about the client, is she hard to work with, will she try to dump the whole project in your lap, will you have the resources to get the job done. Unclear expectations, concerns, anxieties, and preconceptions cloud the atmosphere. In the worst case, downright fears, hard-nosed resistance to technology, and previous bad experience with IS projects may weight the scales in favor of failure. And your job is to build the foundation for what may be months of working together.

PROFILE THE CLIENT

Initial contact gives you an opportunity to accomplish a great deal in a few minutes. To make the most of the opportunity you need to know as much as you can about your client—you need a profile of her and her organization. What is her position in the organization? Her reputation? Her role in relation to other functions? What previous IS projects have involved her function? How successful were they? What are the key business problems of the function she manages? Finding out such information builds your own confidence and improves that crucial first impression on the client.

    A number of sources can be tapped for this information, including organization charts, departmental goal statements, operating plans, friends who work in the department. It is often a good idea to contact the client ahead of the initial meeting and ask if there is material germane to the project that you should examine before the initial meeting. In addition to helping you prepare, this shows the client that you are taking the assignment seriously and are not interested in wasting the client's time. The Client Profile Form (Figure 5–1) includes some key questions you may want to ask about a client. One of the best ways to use this tool is in a team brainstorming session including anyone in the IS group who has had experience in the client's area. If the group comes up with some blanks, they can be filled in through additional research.

A preliminary profile can usually be put together before the initial contact meeting. Test these preliminary assumptions in the meeting, and refine the profile afterward. Pay special attention after the first meeting to the final section of the profile form, listing the major concerns you have about the project. These concerns should be clearly addressed in the contracting stage of the consulting cycle.

The profile can be further expanded and revised as more information is gathered in the contracting and data collection and analysis stages. For more complex projects, especially projects that cut across organizational boundaries, you should develop a partner map, which extends the profile to include other key players and groups affected by the project. Chapter 10 describes the partner map in detail.

FIGURE 5–1
Client Profile Form

Client name _____ Title _____
Client's organization _____ No. of staff _____
Client's direct reports (names & titles) _____
_____
_____
_____
Client's direct supervisor (name & title) _____
What are the client's areas of responsibility? _____
Who are the area's key decision makers, influencers, "rising stars"? ___
_____
_____

FIGURE 5–1—*Concluded*

What relationships (within the area, or with other areas) are important to the project effort? _____

What are the area's key goals? _____

How do these goals tie to overall organizational goals? _____

What is senior management's attitude toward this area? _____

What key factors determine the area's success?
1. _____
2. _____
3. _____
What are the area's major problems or concerns?
1. _____
2. _____
3. _____
What is the client's attitude toward risk? _____

What automation projects have been undertaken in this area? _____

What are the perceptions of these projects in the area? _____

What is the client's technology experience/knowledge level? _____

What technology resources are available to the client area? _____

What other characteristics of the client and his/her area should be taken into consideration in this project? _____

List the main concerns you have entering into this project (key issues to be addressed, key problems you foresee, information necessary to the project that must be verified).
1. _____
2. _____
3. _____
4. _____
5. _____
6. _____
7. _____
8. _____
9. _____
10. _____

No matter how much homework you do, there will be things you simply cannot know about the client. In addition to being prepared, you should also be prepared to be flexible. Keep your antennae up and functioning about the situation and the client. Simply acknowledging that there are all sorts of things you don't know about the client can give you the right attitude going into the meeting.

ESTABLISH RAPPORT WITH THE CLIENT

Once in the initial contact meeting, the consultant should concentrate first on establishing good chemistry for problem solving. There is no set way to do this, no formula that works in all cases. One rule of thumb is to *focus first on the client*. Put all your own concerns aside for awhile and concentrate your attention on the person you will be working with. How can you connect with this person?

One IS consultant had been assigned the most feared client in the organization—a manager with a reputation for snarling intimidation. The consultant reluctantly went to his first meeting, fearing the worst. As he confronted the manager's scowl and shook hands, he noticed a picture of the man fly fishing, with a prize catch on the hook. An avid fisherman himself, the consultant asked about the picture with real interest. The client's eyes lit up, and they were off on a 15-minute discussion of fishing spots. After they had planned a fishing trip for the coming weekend, they settled down to work on the project. The consultant's IS cohorts were dumbfounded when they saw him meet the client in the hall with a warm greeting. The project went smoothly.

Of course, you cannot always be as lucky as this consultant, but knowing something about the interests and work style of a client can be a real help. The key is to remember that building rapport is important. Be aware of the atmosphere of the meeting and the attitude of the client and then act naturally. This may be as simple as discussing a common interest for a minute or two. In other cases, it may involve a brief discussion of your previous experience with the client's functional area or with similar problems. In some cases all that is required is to give undivided attention to the client in order to build a sense that he or she is listened to. If the client obviously has a sense of urgency about the problem, building rapport can mean rolling up your sleeves and diving right into the problem. Whatever the means, the goal is to create the atmosphere for a productive discussion.

LET THE CLIENT KNOW YOU'VE "GOT THE PICTURE"

Gain an understanding of the problem and feed it back to the client. Gory detail is not required at this point; better to feed back a broad-brush analysis stated in solvable terms. The goal is to give the client a sense that you:

- Understand the problem's key elements.
- Are not underestimating its difficulty.
- Are taking it seriously.
- Are interested in solving it.

The most effective way to communicate this understanding is to empathize with the client, step into his or her shoes, and understand what it must be like to have the problem. Understand the emotions and issues surrounding the problem as well as the facts of the problem, and communicate these to the client as well. (See the guidelines for interactive listening in Chapter 11 for help in this process.) Empathy is the key to building the "we" attitude that is at the core of the partnership approach.

PROVIDE A PROBLEM-SOLVING FRAMEWORK

If you are like most IS professionals, you have strong analytical skills. When you really listen to a client's description of a problem, you can analyze that description and provide a problem-solving framework for the problem within 5 or 10 minutes. This does not mean that you understand every nuance of the problem, or that you have a solution already. It means that you have cut the problem up into manageable pieces, put some structure to it, and determined the basic steps needed to proceed. Once you have the picture, you can share that framework using language such as this: "Based on this quick snapshot of your problem, we have a five-step process to go through to reach a solution." Often, sharing this problem-solving framework with the client can help build confidence, clarify the client's understanding of the problem, and put the client at ease.

Before moving on to the contracting stage, ask yourself the following questions:

1. Does the client feel comfortable with me?
2. Is the atmosphere conducive to negotiation on project roles?
3. Do I have a clear understanding of the basic business problem?
4. Does the client feel comfortable with my understanding of the problem?
5. Do I have the information I need to realistically begin negotiations on project issues?

If the answer to any of these questions is no, the initial contact stage is incomplete, and moving on to contracting can be dangerous.

CHAPTER 6

STAGE 2: CONTRACTING

Contracting is the most crucial stage in the entire consulting cycle. Here the framework for the partnership relationship will be established through the sometimes difficult negotiation of goals, roles, and methods. The term *contracting* does not mean that a legalistic document is the goal. In the case of larger projects, some formal documentation may be required by the organization to begin a project, and these documents can be worked up as part of the contracting process. But the intent of this phase is not to "nail people down" or to "cover your rear." Nothing will pull the plug on the beginnings of a partnership relationship faster than making the client feel he or she is being set up with the help of a cover-your-rear contract. The purpose of contracting is to build clarity and mutual agreement on the what, who, when, and how of the project. In addition, contracting is not a one-shot, final event; it is an ongoing, two-way communication process that will be revisited throughout the life of the project.

THREE LEGS MAKE A CONTRACT

This IS consulting contract is like a three-legged stool. As Figure 6–1 shows, the three legs are the client/consultant work relationship, the understanding of the business problem, and the technology that will be used to solve it. If any one of these legs is weak, the contract—and with it the entire project—will fall apart. When this happens, it does no good to point to the two solid, well-turned legs lying on the floor. The stool is a failure. One weak leg is a danger signal that the other two are not as strong as they seem, as Figure 6–1 and Table 6–1 show.

All your skills in the areas outlined in Chapter 2 are subjected to

FIGURE 6–1
Three Legs Make a Contract

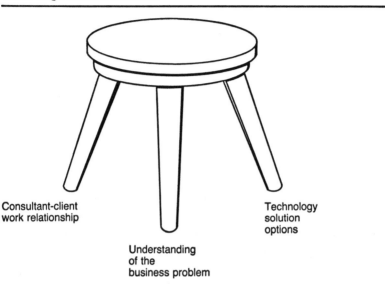

Consultant-client
work relationship

Technology
solution
options

Understanding
of the
business problem

the acid test in the contracting stage—business knowledge, technical knowledge, interpersonal skills, and the consulting-cycle skills that tie them all together. Successful contracting is making sure all three legs are sound. In practice, IS professionals tend to neglect the first leg—the work relationship. This neglect is largely a matter of training; though considerable attention is paid to the process of problem analysis and the technologies used to build solutions, fostering the critical work relationship with the client is usually left to the natural "people skills" of the individual consultant.

CONTRACTING MEANS MUTUAL AGREEMENT

The product of the contracting process is mutual agreement on a number of project issues:

• Parameters/limits of the project. What problems will be addressed by the project? And equally important, what problems will not be addressed?

TABLE 6–1
Impact of Weak Legs on Other Legs

Weak Leg	Impact on Other Legs		
	Work relationship	Understanding of business problem	Technology solution options
Work relationship		Client may withhold key information Client may block consultant efforts Client may avoid in-depth involvement	Client may resist or sabotage implementation Client may discount consultant's solution options Client may not take ownership for solution
Understanding of business problem	Client loses trust due to consultant's lack of understanding Consultant loses credibility		Solution may work but not meet real client needs Solution costs may outweigh benefits Solution may solve immediate problem but fail to address big-picture needs
Technology solution options	Good working relationship may not survive project effort that provides inadequate solution	Business problem will remain unsolved	

• Client's desired results. What are the goals of the project? How does it fit into the client's overall goals? How will the project team know the project is finished? How will the results of the project be evaluated?

• Client/consultant roles. Who will do what? Who will be responsible for what? How will the client and the consultant work together? This is where the ground rules for the partnership relationship are set.

• Deliverables and schedule. The level of detail and completeness of the list of deliverables will vary, but without the list contracting is not complete. Even in very large projects where substantial analysis will be required to set a complete project schedule, a set of next steps and dates should be hammered out as part of the contracting meeting(s) with the client.

• Consultant's needs. What you need from the client is an important part of the contract. This may be commitments of time or resources such

as manpower, facilities, or funds; access to data or operations; or other support activities, such as lobbying senior management.
• Procedures and ground rules. This is the "how" of the contract. A variety of issues can fall into this category, from the type of forms used to gather data to the client's request that a certain person not be dragged into the project. In general, the goal is to ensure that the working relationship runs smoothly by avoiding misunderstanding.

Contracting also prepares the way for all following stages. These stages should be explicitly discussed in the contracting meetings. How will data collection and analysis be handled? Who will be involved? What training requirements are likely? Who will be trained? Who will handle implementation in the client area? What is the time frame for implementation? What are the evaluation criteria for the project, and when should evaluation take place? All these issues are part of the contract and provide both client and consultant with a clearer understanding of the scope and demands of the project. Of course, this is only a preliminary assessment, and changes will occur as the project progresses. Table 6–2 is a contracting checklist that can help to ensure that all the bases are covered.

NEGOTIATING THE CONTRACT

In defining goals, roles, and other aspects of the contract, differences in expectations are sure to arise. Your negotiation skills will come in handy during the contracting process. Two key points to keep in mind during the negotiations:

1. You must maintain a customer-service orientation to the client.
2. You must maintain a careful balance of client/consultant responsibility and commitment.

These two goals often seem at odds when negotiations get tough. Yet navigating the narrow strait between doing-anything-the-client-wants and telling-the-client-what-he-needs-to-do is what successful contracting is all about. To do this effectively you need a consistent negotiating strategy that minimizes the chances of getting off track. Then, you need to carefully monitor the negotiation process in order to recognize and address problems early.

TABLE 6–2
Contracting Checklist

---

1. Is there mutual agreement on the goals of the project effort?
2. How do these goals translate into solvable problems?
3. Are client and consultant roles clear for:
    a. Data collection?
    b. Analysis?
    c. Recommendations?
    d. Decision-making?
    e. Implementation?
    f. Evaluation?
4. Is there provision for follow-up and evaluation so that both parties can learn from the project?
    a. What is the agreed upon evaluation method?
    b. What are the evaluation criteria?
5. Are all parties to the contract involved in the contracting process? If not, what other parties should be included?
6. What agreement exists on sharing responsibility for the project?
7. Are the requests and promises made realistic?
8. What agreement exists that the client's desired results are really needed:
    a. In the client's organization?
    b. In the consultant's organization?
9. Is the contract freely entered by both parties without coercion or misgivings?
10. Does the contract allow for renegotiation and necessary change along the way?

MAKE DEPOSITS BEFORE
YOU MAKE WITHDRAWALS

Most banks will not let you withdraw money before you have made a deposit. Most clients are the same way. They do not want to give up their precious staff, time, and dollar resources to you until they see you putting something tangible on the table for them. You want to end up with a contract that includes roughly equal commitments from you and the client, but you will rarely achieve this by asking the client to make all his or her commitments first. You do not want to be in the vulnerable position of offering support if the client is not willing to commit necessary resources to the project. But the client is at least as vulnerable as you are, and needs to feel comfortable that it is worth it to commit those resources.

A simple negotiating strategy can minimize these problems:

1. Client requirements.
2. Consultant offers.
3. Consultant requirements.
4. Client offers.

We can't overemphasize the importance of this little plan. One of the most common mistakes in the contracting process is starting off with a set of demands on the client. Some IS consultants, in an honest effort to get out of the technical wizard role and into partnership with clients, push to get firm commitments of client time and resources before negotiating their own role in the project. This can lead to stiff resistance, especially those who have been trained into dependence on IS through the years of working with technical wizards.

PRACTICAL NEGOTIATION STRATEGIES

The consultant/client discussions and negotiations during contracting demand good communications skills. The following rules of negotiation can help you improve your contracting skills.

When you want something, ask for it in direct, positive language. Firmness and confidence are real consulting assets. Stating needs in wishy-washy terms in order not to offend the client will not only make the client less likely to take the request seriously; it will also undermine his or her confidence in your ability to get the job done. Avoid negative prejudgments ("She won't like this, but . . ."). You cannot convince the client if you are not convinced yourself. When you make a request, avoid negative language ("I don't know if you can do this, but . . ."). Instead, preface the request with benefits and sound reasons, and provide a plan that makes it as simple as possible for the client to respond positively.

You can say almost anything to a client when following five simple rules:

1. Sincerely consider the client's point of view.
2. Be forthright and take responsibility for the message even when there is concern that it may create conflict.
3. Speak in a nonthreatening conversational tone.

4. Be sure about the facts.
5. Think through how to present the information first.

Work toward firm commitments on who will do what, and when. A good tool for this is a simple task list, with columns for task description, task accountability, and completion date. As with all contracting methods, it is designed to be used as a working tool, not a means of enforcing commitments. Using this chart, work with the client to develop a list of tasks. Listing tasks first enables you to develop a sense of teamwork on the project by focusing attention on the tasks before addressing the more sensitive issue of resource allocation, where negotiation is usually required.

When necessary, offer a compromise. Your responsibility in the contracting process is to keep your eye on the goal, which is to serve the client in the solution of the client's problem. In difficult situations, the ability to identify and offer a compromise can be a powerful negotiating tool.

TEST THE AGREEMENT

As the contracting negotiations progress, test the client's level of comfort and commitment to the agreement. Ignoring client uneasiness or reticence in order to move forward more quickly may seem like a time saver, but in the long run it will usually create wasted effort and delays ten or a hundred times as long as the time saved. Invest the time up front to avoid those painful readjustments and changes in direction later.

No matter how much care is taken in the contracting process, unforeseen problems and a changing work environment guarantee that you will need to loop back to the contracting stage one or more times as the project progresses. Your job is not to nail down the perfect contract, but to minimize the size of the loops. Here is a checklist of hints on testing the agreement:

- Pay attention to the client's reactions as the negotiations proceed.
- Empathize, trying to see your proposals as the client would see them.
- Watch for body language that expresses concern or confusion, or conflicts with the client's words.

- Listen for signs of concern, confusion, anxiety, lack of trust and confidence in the client's tone of voice.
- Listen to your own intuition about how the client is feeling.
- Check the energy level of the discussion. When it drops, the client may have unexpressed concerns.
- Use open-ended, neutral questions (for example, "Do any other issues or concerns come to mind as we walk through these first five tasks?") to give the client an opportunity to express concerns.
- Check how eager your client is to move on to the next step.
- Watch how your client follows through on the first few commitments of resource or time to the project.

Most IS consultants can perform this testing very well, if they build it into their plan and pay attention to the signs. Nevertheless, you may come out of a contracting meeting feeling that something went wrong, though exactly what is unclear. A good strategy in this situation is to sit with a trusted consulting associate and walk through the meeting, describing what happened, and letting the associate react. Doing this can shed light on your own blind spots, and enable you to go back to the client and get things back on track.

Another tool for testing is the follow-up memo after the contracting session. This memo should touch all the bases covered in the meeting, for the purpose of ensuring mutual agreement. The difference between a cover-your-rear memo and a testing memo is that the testing memo is followed up by a visit or phone call to make sure the memo is on track, with an openness to renegotiation where necessary. Figure 6–2 is a sample follow-up memo at the end of this chapter.

MAINTAIN COMMUNICATION
WITH YOUR CLIENT

Finally, it is the process, not the product, of contracting that is important. And that process does not end with the production of a task list and schedule. Contracting is an ongoing communication process, and maintaining that communication should be part of your routine. Parts of the contract will change, and renegotiation may be necessary. Your goal is not to prevent change, but to ensure that all involved parties (including you!) are aware of and agree to the change.

FIGURE 6-2
Sample Contracting Follow-Up Memo

TO: D. Hanfield

FROM: J. O'Keefe

SUBJECT: New Marketing Database Project

DATE: April 20

Don, I enjoyed getting together with you Wednesday to clarify goals and roles for the new marketing project. I've prepared the attached summary of my understanding of our discussion, and will contact you Thursday, 4/23 to make sure we're in tune. If you have questions or concerns about any items, or see anything I've omitted, we can discuss it then.

Thanks for your attention to these details, Don; I want to make sure we are starting off with a clear picture of your needs and constraints and with agreement on how we will work together on the project. We're eager to begin work and I am confident that the project team we have assembled will do a first-rate job. Should you want to talk to me before Thursday, contact my office.

J. O'Keefe

1. Business Goals of the Project

Improve sales personnel effectiveness in dealing with large potential customer base for Hitek I and II units. Salespeople need quick access before and during sales trips to data such as:

- Potential customers in a particular geographical area.
- Current customers by geographical area/industry.
- Date of last contact with customer.
- Key contacts at customer locations.
- Likelihood of buying based on previous contacts.
- Status of in-process orders.

A full set of specifications for data required will be gathered as part of the project.

Success of the project will be indicated in part by feedback from sales personnel regarding ability to maximize payoff of a given sales trip by visiting more potential buyers and using data to focus efforts where sales are most likely. Preliminary interviews indicate potential to increase sales of these units by 10 percent within one year for a revenue boost of

FIGURE 6–2—*Continued*

$600,000. Actual sales figures will be linked with sales personnel feedback to evaluate project payoff.

2. Scope of the Project

Only the Hitek I and II product lines, and the eight sales personnel assigned to them, will be covered. The Hitek III+ and other product lines will not be included in this project effort, though a follow-up may be scheduled to expand the scope of the system next year if this effort is successful.

3. Resources

Marketing budgets at this time allow a $100,000 outlay for capital on this project. Involvement by marketing personnel is as follows:

J. Torres	Project Leader	4 hours/week
T. Wills	Sales Rep.	4 hours/week
G. Florio	Marketing Staff	8 hours/week
R. Giles	Clerical Support	8 hours/week

You agreed to brief T. Wills, who could not attend our meeting, by Thursday on her involvement to make sure she is on board with our plans. The following IS personnel will be assigned to the project:

J. O'Keefe	Project Leader
E. Stein	Technical Support
R. Ziff	Database Analyst
B. Taylor	Training

4. Phase 1

The following tasks have been identified and preliminary assignments made:

1. Define data needs:
   a. T. Wills and G. Florio, Marketing, J. O'Keefe, IS—will interview sales representatives to build consensus on what data is required.
2. Research solution options:
   a. R. Ziff, IS—will investigate database options for storing the data and providing easy inquiry.
   b. E. Stein, IS—will investigate telecommunications access options for sales people in field.
   c. T. Wills, Marketing—will work with E. Stein to test and evaluate access options.

FIGURE 6–2—*Concluded*

3. Prepare report on data requirements and solution options:
   a. J. Torres, Marketing—Prepare report based on input from team members above.
   b. R. Giles, Marketing—Produce and distribute report

5. Phase I Due Dates

Data requirements to J. Torres, R. Ziff, E. Stein	5/7
Technical options to J. Torres	5/14
Report distribution to team members	5/18
Meeting to review data requirements and solution options	5/20

At the 5/20 meeting, the project team will outline the solution and explain the technical options and costs. Your decision at this meeting will determine whether we move forward with development. We estimate approximately 25 hours of consulting time before this meeting billed against your budget at our standard rate.

6. Phase 2

With your go-ahead, we will then proceed with the following tasks (lead responsibility for each, per our discussion, is indicated by the initials following the task):

1. Development of database structure/files	RZ
2. Development of inquiry procedures	GF
3. Ordering of equipment/software	ES
4. Installation/testing of equipment/software	ES
5. Collection of existing data from sales personnel	GF
6. Data entry of existing sales data	RG
7. Implementation of system	TW/ES
8. Training for sales personnel and support staff	TW/BT
9. Postimplementation evaluation of system	JT/JO
10. Six-month evaluation	JT/JO
11. Discussion of follow-up project	Team

An estimate of IS labor costs and project schedule for Phase 2 will be developed one week after your go-ahead. J. Torres and I will meet weekly throughout the project to discuss progress and will brief you at your weekly staff meeting.

CHAPTER 7

STAGE 3: DATA COLLECTION AND ANALYSIS

Once you and your client have put together a solid contract, the task of collecting and evaluating detailed information about the business problem begins. Gathering and analyzing data is one of the most familiar tasks for most IS professionals. Turning a business procedure into logical steps that can be coded into programming language has been the bread and butter of systems analysts for nearly 30 years. Your challenge as an IS consultant is to use the data collection and analysis process as another tool for building partnership and joint responsibility for the project.

DATA COLLECTION METHODS

Seven basic methods can be used to collect data:

1. Surveys. Sending out a form polling a large number of people on project-related issues.
2. Interviews. Discussions with one or more client personnel on project issues.
3. Focus groups. A more formalized approach that entails a task force of client and nonclient personnel assembled to gather and analyze data on the project.
4. Data sampling. Examining reports, forms, and other documents and data items used by the client.
5. Direct observations. Watching the workflow in the client organization.
6. Prototyping. Developing a quick "straw man" system that will be refined through a number of iterations with the client.

7. Intuition. Using your own instincts to build a picture of what is going on in the client organization.

Any one method has strengths and weaknesses, and should be used in combination with other methods. Table 7–1 summarizes the benefits, concerns, and best cross-checks for each of these methods.

Several of these methods, in particular interviews and focus groups, involve in-depth interaction with the client and other project members. This interaction is an opportunity for building partnership.

BUILDING TRUST AND MOTIVATION DURING DATA COLLECTION

Skill in gathering information is not the only criterion for success in the data collection meeting. The level of the client's trust in you and his or her motivation to participate in the project will have a major impact on the partnership relationship as well as on the quality of the information you obtain. IS consulting projects—which almost always involve changes to work processes, new and unfamiliar technology, new training requirements, and (at least temporary) loss of control—are full of potential for distrust and resistance. To ensure that all your hard work gets put to use, your consulting efforts should be designed from the start to boost the client's trust and motivation.

Show the Client He or She Is in Capable Hands

Clients who feel they are in the hands of a competent, professional consultant will be more comfortable providing information. You can build this reputation in a number of ways: selective reference to your track record, discussion of a previous project with some similarities, approaching the meeting with energy and proper preparation. But do not assume that your client does not need this assurance. Even a good consulting reputation can be undermined by consultant behavior that does not instill confidence.

Be Direct and Honest in Communicating with the Client

You want the client to be open in sharing facts and feelings about the project. Yet asking the client to be honest and open usually doesn't do any good. Modeling that openness yourself, on the other hand, is one of

TABLE 7–1
Summary of Data Collection Methods

Data Collection Method	Strengths	Concerns	Best Cross-Checks
Surveys	Timesaving for gathering information from large groups Can often be quantified and analyzed	Easily misinterpreted Difficult to design effective questions Miss background, context, emotions, nonverbal cues	Interviews/meetings Focus groups Direct observation
Interviews/Meetings	Most opportunity to work on client/consultant relationship Most opportunity to understand client concerns, emotions, issues about project	Time-consuming Demands most consulting skills	Direct observation Data sampling Intuition
Focus Groups	Promote partnership Encourage multiple perspectives Visible indicator of management support for project	Difficult to form, maintain Time-consuming May not raise sensitive issues in group setting	Direct observation Data sampling Interviews/meetings Intuition
Data Sampling	Analyze currently used data in client organization Provides objective view of workflow	Must view data in context of workflow and actual use	Interviews/meetings Direct observation
Direct Observations	Provides objective view of workflow	Observed personnel may change behavior Observed slice of time may not be typical	Interviews/meetings Data sampling
Prototyping	Provides client something concrete to evaluate Design is built in partnership with client Client educated in design process	Time-consuming Some prototype systems use excessive system resources	Interviews/meetings Data sampling Direct observation
Intuition	Can perceive issues client is not comfortable discussing	Must be checked against concrete facts	Interviews/meetings Direct observations

the best tools you have. If the client sees that you are honest even when it is uncomfortable, he or she will feel less need to second guess what you say, and to filter what he or she tells you about the project. On the other hand, if the client senses that you have a hidden agenda, the client's guard will go up.

Communicate Your Commitment to the Client

Joe, a systems analyst for a large insurance firm, had been assigned to a new systems development project already underway in the Life Insurance group. The initial data collection meeting had already been scheduled. Joe was not particularly enthused about this project, because it represented an almost impossible addition to his already huge workload. Being a dedicated worker, however, he sandwiched the initial data collection meeting with the manager of the Life department between meetings for two other projects. As so often happens, Joe's first meeting took longer than expected, and it was a difficult one to boot. Joe arrived 10 minutes late for his meeting with the new client and was obviously preoccupied and rushed as he began asking questions. His impatience with the additional workload showed in his attitude, and the client felt he was barely being listened to.

When, halfway through the meeting, Joe began to check his watch in anticipation of the next meeting, the client broke in and suggested that perhaps the meeting would be more effective if held at another time. Joe was grateful, and apologized for the time squeeze. When Joe offered to reschedule for next week, the client suggested that he would call Joe early next week to set a time. Joe hurried on to the next meeting, feeling happy that he had finally met a client with a sense of IS's tough workload. When he got back to his office, however, he faced a concerned project leader, who told him that the client had called to suggest that if IS was not committed to the project, his group was not going to waste its time.

Showing your client that you are on board, that you have made a real commitment to solving his or her problem builds trust. How could Joe have put this rule into practice in his difficult situation? Obviously, he could not stuff more hours into his already hectic day. On reflection, he realized that his frustration with being assigned to yet another project had kept him from treating the new client's problem as important. Treating it as important, he realized with hindsight, would have meant taking seriously the time conflict he had and either rescheduling the already scheduled meeting, or talking with the client ahead of time to negotiate a shorter meeting that would fit into his packed schedule and then a longer meeting when more time was available.

Also, treating the problem as important meant putting his frustrations behind him when he met with that client and communicating his commitment to the project rather than his frustrations. For he was committed—he was known in his group for hard work and dedication. But his failure to communicate that dedication almost lost his team a client.

Communicate an Agenda in Advance

Mary, project leader on a development project that crossed several department boundaries, called a project meeting on short notice. Unknown to the client, Mary invited Mike, who worked in another department involved in the project, to provide a perspective on that group's interface with the proposed system. Unknown to Mary, the client had had a serious disagreement with Mike on an issue related to the project with this staffer two days before. As the client sat down, Mary began to discuss this issue and ask the client's opinion on several aspects. Because of a key staffer's absence on vacation, the client was unable to answer the questions. Mike sat across the table and shook his head.

Any management course will tout the benefits of an agenda for keeping a meeting organized and saving time. For the IS consultant, the benefits in building client trust are at least as important. Part of the IS profession's earned bad reputation is that we surprise and confuse our users: we talk a different language, we lord our technical knowledge over clients, we fit their problems to our technologies. The religious use of an agenda for every project-related meeting can help reverse that reputation. Even if the meeting is a brief one-on-one, with only a few points to cover, an agenda is a must. Mary's story may be an extreme example, but the issues it raises are all too common. Communicating an agenda in advance:

- Communicates respect for the client.
- Shows that you will not risk embarrassing the client.
- Enables the client to identify others who should be present at the meeting to ensure that you get the necessary information.

- Gives the client time to do necessary preparatory work.
- Allows the client to delete or add items to the agenda before the meeting, which in turn enables you to use your own preparation time more efficiently.

The result of communicating the agenda in advance is a jointly developed blueprint for the meeting—and this is problem-solving partnership in action. Nothing will do more for building client ownership of the project. The strategy is simple: prepare and communicate the meeting agenda far enough in advance for the client to examine it and respond before the meeting. A good time to check on the agenda is when calling the day before to reconfirm the meeting. Test the client's reaction to the agenda and revise it if necessary.

What about impromptu meetings? What about all the times you don't have a chance to prepare? Even in these situations you can work up an agenda in the five minutes it takes to walk to the meeting, and then list the points on a blackboard or flipchart. The client still has a chance to react to them, perhaps to put one or two items off to a later time, and to provide input.

What about the times when you are called into someone else's meeting, and that person hasn't prepared an agenda? You can still play an important role by asking for one, right at the start. You can even offer to write the key points on the board, and act as facilitator to keep the meeting on track. All these things build trust by showing the client that you are organized, results-oriented, and absolutely uninterested in wasting the client's time. Of course, your own time is not wasted either, and you are much more likely to get the information needed for the project.

Provide Immediate Client Benefit

The data collection meeting is not just a process of pulling information from the client. Rather, it is a two-way communication with the work relationship at the center:

Consultant obtains ◄——————— Client/Consultant ———————► Client gets
   information   work relationship   immediate
                                                 benefit

We're not sure whether it is part of IS professionals' temperament or training that makes us so willing to put patient months of exacting technical effort into a project before we see the payoff in results. For some IS professionals, the process of watching a system grow is reward enough over the long months of a large project. Whatever it is that gives us this saintly patience with the slow process of bringing a new system to birth, our clients seldom share it. Even the manager of Strategic Planning is motivated more by what is going on this week than by what is promised next year. Facing a major project effort, clients see the demands on their time and resources much more clearly than the promised benefits, which may be months or even years away.

Promising a big payoff six months down the road for all the hard work the client is doing is not nearly as effective as providing a small but real benefit at each step along the way. You can keep client motivation high simply by making sure the client has something at the end of each meeting that he or she didn't have at the beginning. One IS group we know of has as its motto, "We add value to every transaction." And they don't mean machine transactions, they mean human transactions. Everything from a major project review meeting to a chance meeting in the cafeteria. Immediate benefits can take many forms. Here are some examples:

- Feeding back to the client some information gathered by the project team that enables the client to understand the problem better.
- Identifying and delivering some benefits quickly—such as reducing the processing cycle on the existing system while developing the new one.
- Teaching the client something of value—providing an overview of database technology in nontechnical terms that reduces the client's uncertainty about the project.
- Providing some genuine, realistic assurance in an area where the client is concerned about failure.

The benefit need not always be project related. Most IS consultants have a broad exposure to the organization that gives them regular contact with organizationwide issues that many clients lack. Serving as an information link for your client, giving them some intelligence about developments in another department that may have impact in their area, can be just as effective.

Test your effectiveness in following this rule after your next client meeting by asking yourself what your client has after the meeting that he or she didn't have before. If the only answer is "a headache," don't be surprised if your client's motivation starts to drop!

CONTROLLING DATA COLLECTION MEETINGS

It is your responsibility to *control* data collection meetings with the informed consent of the client. This does not mean being dictatorial. It does not mean making sure that everyone in the meeting does or thinks or says as the person in control wishes. Controlling a meeting means facilitating.

Take Facilitative Control

As a facilitator, your responsibilities are:

- Making sure the meeting is productive.
- Keeping it on track with the shared agenda.
- Clarifying misunderstandings.
- Ensuring that each participant gets a chance to contribute.
- Reformulating counterproductive personal attacks in neutral language.
- Restating negative statements as solvable problems.
- Making sure the meeting is closed effectively and that action assignments and follow-ups are clear.

Most clients will be happy to have you take this responsibility. For many it is a relief to know that someone is organized and enthusiastic enough to manage the meeting. In fact, it can be a real builder of trust and motivation. Of course, it is important to handle it correctly. In most cases all this requires is announcing as part of the opening that you will act as facilitator to keep the meeting on track.

Base Your Control on the Agenda

One way to turn taking control into a problem is to work without an agenda. Control should always be based on the agenda you and your client have agreed on in advance. The agenda gives everyone a guideline to follow, and the facilitator's role is simply to keep the group to the guideline.

Chapters 12 and 13 describe additional tools that are helpful in the data collection phase of the consulting cycle.

CHAPTER 8

STAGES 4 AND 5:
RECOMMENDATIONS AND
DECISION MAKING

Stage 4 begins when data collection and analysis have provided sufficient information to define options for technical solutions. As in the earlier stages, our emphasis is on using this stage to continue to build partnership with the client, in preparation for the client's role in decision making about the basic direction to be taken with the project. The following rules will increase your success in this stage.

LINK RECOMMENDATIONS CLEARLY
TO THE CLIENT'S PROBLEM

Ensure that the recommendations explicitly address the key aspects of the problems identified and verified in the contracting and data collection/analysis stages. It is a good idea to begin a recommendations presentation or meeting with a crisp review of these key aspects of the problem to reaffirm the mutual understanding and make clear that the recommendations were based on it.

PRESENT SOLUTION OPTIONS
FOR CLIENT REVIEW

Whenever appropriate, present two or more solution options. Options might involve different technologies (for example, mainframe computer system versus networked personal computers), different implementations of the same technology (a full-system pilot followed by full implementation versus a phased implementation across the user base), buy versus make decisions for software packages, different timetables, different features, and so on. The description of each option, moreover, should include a clear picture of what each requires in the remaining stages of the cycle.

Presenting solution options has several benefits. First, it helps open up your thinking to consider various alternatives. One of the biggest dangers in IS consulting is the narrowness of focus that comes from knowing a small set of technologies well. This tunnel vision traps even the best IS professionals. Since it is difficult for any one IS consultant to know a wide range of technologies and development tools in depth, it is wise to get several IS consultants involved in identifying solution options. All options presented should clearly address the key aspects of the problem; don't present options that are seriously deficient simply to have more than one option to present.

MAKE SURE THE OPTIONS ARE CLEAR TO THE CLIENT

The presentation to the client should clearly define how the options address the client's needs and concerns. One simple way to do this is to create a chart that lists the key advantages and disadvantages of each solution option. If several options or a long list of decision criteria are involved, it may be helpful to structure this information graphically. Figure 8–1 does this using a decision gate method.

For very complex projects, computer-based decision-support tools can automate this type of comparison. These tools typically automate a weighted-criteria decision matrix, helping the user rank alternatives against user-defined criteria and weight the criteria based on importance, to determine a total point value for each option. Such tools make it easy to modify assumptions, compare options, and create graphic displays of the results. Whatever method is used, make sure the assumptions involved are clearly understood and supported by the client. The decision gate chart (Figure 8–1) uses numbered descriptions to make the decision criteria as explicit as possible.

FIGURE 8–1
Decision Gate Chart for a Project Management System

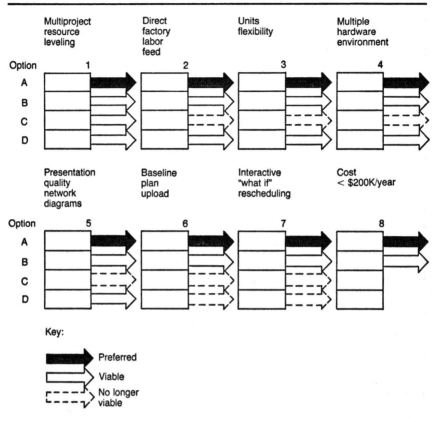

Key to Decision Points:

1. System must be able to balance project personnel resources over multiple projects, with some personnel working on more than one project.

2. System must accept input in machine-readable form with minimal conversion effort from factory floor bar-code touch labor system.

3. System must enable scheduling resources by hour, day, week interchangeably.

4. System must run on IBM 30xx/MVS, Digital Equipment VAX/VMS, and UNIX environments.

5. System must enable preparation of color, presentation-quality network diagrams in large format on existing graphics output devices for customer review purposes.

6. System must accept input of baseline plans with task definition and resource assignments from currently used PC-based system.

7. System must allow examination of rescheduling options with on-screen viewing of resulting impact.

8. System costs must be under $200,000/year, including license, training for eight schedulers/year, and support.

PRESENTING YOUR RECOMMENDATIONS

To prepare for your recommendations presentation, step into your client's shoes, and revisit your client profile. Of course, you now have much more data to work with. What are the client's main concerns coming into this meeting? Whatever they are, the presentation had better address them clearly. If the project effort has been effective so far, and the prior stages of the cycle worked well, the recommendations should come as no surprise to the client; but the bases must still be covered so that the client feels comfortable.

The actual recommendations meeting or presentation to the client will call on all your presentation skills. Communicate confidence by your body language, words, tone, and organization of the material. Reaffirm your commitment to solving the client's problem.

MAKE THE CLIENT COMFORTABLE ENOUGH WITH THE TECHNOLOGY TO MAKE AN INFORMED DECISION

In this phase you will discuss technical specifics, perhaps for the first time in the consulting cycle. Factor in your client's level of comfort and familiarity with the technologies, and do not run the risk of losing the client in a trail of acronyms or jargon. This stage demands patience, sensitivity to client confusion, and a willingness to invest some time educating the client. How many times do we complain that our clients do not understand the technologies well enough to do their part on a project? And yet who will they learn from if not from us?

This phase also demands the ability to talk about technical solutions in nontechnical terms, to explain how the solution meets the business needs in language that is immediately understandable to the client. A good strategy for avoiding problems in this area is to practice the recommendations presentation in front of a non-IS friend to get some objective feedback about the language used.

OBJECTIVELY DESCRIBE THE PROS AND CONS OF THE OPTIONS

What if you think that one option is clearly superior? Isn't it your job to communicate this to the client? It seems logical, since the consultant is in most cases more knowledgeable in the technology than the client. But this approach has dangers. First, it assumes that you are free of biases that might result in a wrong decision. Second, it assumes your knowledge of the technology makes you more qualified to assess the appropriateness of the technology to the client's particular circumstances. Even where you have done an outstanding job of building partnership and getting into the client's shoes, this approach may cause problems.

If the client is confident and not intimidated by your knowledge of the technology, he or she will argue against your choice, and you will have set up a conflict. If the client lacks confidence in dealing with technologies, or lacks interest in getting involved with technical details, he or she will be hesitant to disagree with your recommendation despite concerns about its applicability. And if the client goes along with your recommendation without understanding or agreeing, the resulting system will be "the consultant's" system, and responsibility for successful implementation and use will likely be dropped in your lap. If the client follows your recommendations and the project fails—for whatever reason—you suffer the disadvantage of the technical wizard role by taking the blame for failure.

Your technical expertise must be used in this phase, but in clearly and objectively outlining the pros and cons of the options for the client. If you do this job well, and the client agrees with the pros and cons and doesn't see any problems that the consultant missed, the client will in all probability select the option the consultant prefers. If the client does see additional problems, they can be brought out onto the table and worked into the decision process without straining the consultant's credibility. In either case partnership is fostered by involving the client in the process.

For the same reasons it is dangerous to tip the scales in favor of a certain option by the way the options are presented. Your objectivity and impartiality must be genuine, or the results will be the same as if you had openly recommended one option. This ploy can cause even more trouble because the effect is insidious: the client will sense the pressure toward a certain option, though he or she may not be fully conscious of it.

What if the organization's standards or operating environment limit you to only one solution option, or two or more, none of which is applicable? Even here, it is not in your or the project's interest to recommend something because it is the only thing available. There is nothing to be gained by recommending an available technology that has a high risk of not satisfying the client's needs. This only damages IS's credibility, wastes resources, and frustrates another client. If what is available is really not applicable, you have a responsibility to be forthright and tell the client that you do not have a solution.

With clients' increasing flexibility in bringing in end-user computing solutions without IS's help, however, it pays for the IS consultant to be as open as possible in examining options, even if they are outside the standard offerings of the IS function. If the clients perceive IS only as a roadblock and an enforcer of rigid standards, they are less likely to come to IS for advice, and more likely to chart their own course without IS's expertise.

We find real resistance on this issue on the part of many experienced, highly skilled IS professionals. And for good reason. This is the point in the cycle where the IS consultant's sincerity in seeking partnership is tested. Are you really serious about letting go of the technical wizard role? Are you really interested in working as consultants in solving the organization's business problems? Can you avoid the force-fit mentality that is so damaging to IS's reputation?

We are not advocating technical anarchy, where 20 different technologies that do the same job are brought in just because users asked for them. Nor are we advocating the philosophy we call "If that's what they want" in which the IS consultant "reluctantly" gives in to a user recommendation that IS does not believe in, sits by and watches the solution fail, and then stands sagely over the ruins saying, "I knew it wouldn't work." Both of these approaches miss the mark of building partnership.

Of course, it is significant that a particular technology is in place and fully supported, while another is not. But if you routinely use these criteria to avoid even considering other technologies, then you are working with blinders on. These blinders have led too many organizations to write IS off as a key player. "Already installed and supported" is an important factor when selecting a solution option and should be communicated to the client; however, here, as in so many aspects of consulting, how something is said is as important as what is said.

The first step is to see the issue from the client's point of view, not IS's. "We in IS already know this product" and "We in IS will not have to learn a new tool" are not client benefits. They are self-serving and will appear so to the client. However, "Our in-house expertise in this product would likely reduce the development time by six weeks," or "We have these terminals in stock, which would cut lead time for delivery," or "Our lack of expertise on this technology would require the use of external contractors at an estimated cost of $100,000," might be appropriate issues for a particular client—but only if they accurately address real client concerns. A solid understanding of the client's point of view and genuine objectivity in researching and communicating the pros and cons of solution options are critical.

Openness and objectivity in considering and laying out solution options has another benefit: it gives you the flexibility necessary for creativity in meeting business needs. Technical blinders can keep you from seeing a solution outside your normal focus that could make you and IS heroes in the organization. In one large manufacturing company, IS was heavily focused on major multiyear systems development projects and, though they were producing successful systems, they suffered from the image of delivering solutions so slowly that the business had changed in the meantime.

This reputation changed literally overnight when someone in marketing came to IS for help with competitive analysis, and an IS consultant identified an off-the-shelf software package for marketing support that was user-operated and required little support from IS. This inexpensive package was a huge success, with real impact on the organization's ability to respond to market trends. With minimal expenditure of resources, IS's position and visibility in the organization improved dramatically.

Taking off the blinders often has another benefit for you, the consultant. It can build new enthusiasm as your technical horizons are broadened. Your talents are challenged in real analysis of the tools available and not focused on using your single technological hammer on whatever problem comes along. Of course, this role is a larger one than that of the technician role and requires exposure to the market and to new technologies. Not every IS professional will respond favorably to this change; some prefer to remain technicians with a specific expertise, and these people are valuable resources. The effective IS function needs a balance between these technicians and consultants who thrive on the broader challenge of meeting client needs.

In addition to IS resistance on this issue, we also find real opposition to client decision making on the client side. Over the years we in IS have trained clients to give IS this responsibility, and some clients are likely to see your attempts to change the situation as pushing more work on them. Some clients will face this new responsibility with anxiety since they are not comfortable with the technologies involved. These concerns must be addressed through patience, education, and success. One surefire method of *increasing* client concerns and anxieties is to not let them know that they will be the decision makers until it is time to make the decision. These issues must be part of the contracting discussion, and client concerns about technology should be addressed by discussing your responsibility for clarifying options in the recommendation stage in language the client can understand.

Stage 5, decision making, is the shortest stage in the consulting cycle, but it is the pivotal point in the process. If you have successfully laid the groundwork in the first four stages and the client selects an option with confidence and comfort, the rest of the project has a high chance of success.

DECISION MAKING IS THE CLIENT'S STAGE

The client has to live with the solution. The partnership process and the consulting cycle recognize this by allowing the client control over his or her own destiny. Not that you are passive here—your role is to provide all the information needed to make an informed decision, clarify issues, and ensure that the client is comfortable with the decision.

CLIENT OPTIONS INCLUDE "NO" AND "NONE OF THE ABOVE"

What if the client does not select one of the options presented? In some cases decision making can be a go/no-go judgment; the team has not found a cost-effective solution that meets the client's needs. This result is not necessarily a failure of the consulting process. It may be that the goals the client wants to achieve are not worth the investment given the current state of technology. If partnership has been built along the way, the client will see that you have played a valuable role in clarifying this issue and not go away feeling that IS has failed to deliver.

The decision-making process may also result in a decision that none of the options presented is appropriate but that further work is needed. The investigation done in the recommendation stage may bring to light some issues that require looping back to do more data collection or even recontracting to attack the problem in a different way. This result is not a failure either; it is better to loop back from this stage than to wait until after a solution is implemented and found to be ineffective. The goal, again, is to keep the loops as small as possible to avoid wasting resources and time.

TEST CLIENT COMFORT AND COMMITMENT TO THE SOLUTION

Don't treat this stage as a hurdle that must be jumped before getting on with the project. Don't pressure the client to make a decision quickly. It has become a cliche that U.S. business culture tends to rush the front end of the decision process and make up for it by correcting problems after implementation, whereas Japanese business culture spends the time up front to build real agreement so that implementation runs smoothly. Because our cultural bias runs this way, it is helpful to exert some energy in the other direction: to deliberately go slow in the decision-making stage.

Use all your instincts to test the client's commitment and comfort regarding the decision. Is there a feeling that the bases are covered and the project is ready to proceed? Or does the client appear reticent? Does he or she have enthusiasm for the solution, or an "I guess it's the best we can do" attitude? The same methods for determining that the contract was on target (see stage 2) should be used to ensure that the decision to proceed is solid.

CHAPTER 9

STAGES 6 THROUGH 9: DELIVERING BUSINESS SOLUTIONS

With decision making, the foundations of partnership are firmly built. But the partnership process is by no means complete. The work relationship with the client must be managed throughout the project. Many of the techniques described in the first five stages apply in the remaining five stages. This chapter describes partnership concerns and techniques specific to stages 6 through 9 of the cycle.

STAGE 6—DEVELOPMENT, ASSISTANCE, AND TRAINING

In system development projects, this stage includes the detailed design phase where most of the actual development work is done. In end-user computing projects, the client's organization may be responsible for the actual development, with the IS consultant providing support, problem resolution, and guidance, and arranging for necessary training. The work involved in this stage should come as no surprise to the client if the previous stages are handled effectively. Roles in this stage should have been discussed in general in the contracting stage, and in detail in the recommendations and decision-making phases.

Maintain Communication with Your Client

Maintaining partnership at this stage is largely a matter of maintaining communication. There may be weeks of time during system development when no input is needed from the client. In end-user computing projects where the client is responsible for development, it is easy for you to slip into a passive role and wait for the client to call. Both parties have reason to keep the flow of communication going in order to avoid wasting resources. Whatever the roles on a particular project, you should take the initiative in maintaining this communication.

Use Training to Build Partnership

Training is an often neglected part of the partnership-building process. It can be one of IS's most effective tools in building good relationships with clients, or one of the weakest links in the partnership. Make the person or persons providing the training for the project (whether they are client or IS personnel) part of the project team, with particular involvement at the contracting stage, when a rough sketch of training requirements should be made, and after the decision-making stage, when detailed training plans and course development or acquisition should begin. The more closely involved the trainer is with the project and the client, the more effective he or she will be in using training to build partnership.

Use the Trainer as a Feedback Loop

If he or she is made a true partner in the project, the trainer can be positioned as a neutral third party who can provide an objective ear for the eventual users of the new system. Some users will raise concerns about the new system to a trainer that they would not share with a project leader or consultant. These concerns can be valuable indicators of flaws in the system. And as the project moves on to the implementation stage, where users are trained in depth, the trainer is in the best position to give the project team feedback on what is working and what isn't, where there is resistance and where things are running smoothly. A trainer who has been involved in the project can be a real asset at this point and can help save a project that runs into trouble.

STAGE 7—IMPLEMENTATION

Much has been written about the technical and logistical aspects of system implementation. It is the stage where most system failures become visible. It is also the stage where the effectiveness of the partnership is tested. From the partnership standpoint, one rule can increase your effectiveness at this stage.

Implementation Is the Client's Responsibility

This is true whether the project is an end-user developed system or a large-scale IS development project. The users of the system should see it as an effort based in their area, not a system being imposed on them from outside. Of course, your job is to support the client in planning and executing the implementation. The level of involvement by the client and his or her staff is usually a reliable indicator of project success.

Build Support for the Solution

In implementation, your skills as a change agent are tested. Installing the system successfully and training those who must use it are only half the battle. The other half is building support for and confidence in the solution. The larger the population that will use the new system, the larger this aspect of the job becomes. It is part public relations, part marketing, and all consulting. It is also an area where many IS professionals feel uncomfortable. Their technical background conditions them to an environment where things either work or don't work. They are not generally interested in the people side of change management, where feelings, concerns for power and risk and job security, fear of change, and a Pandora's box full of other annoyingly human issues come into play. Yet this is exactly where so many systems efforts fail.

A classic example involved a senior vice president who relied heavily on a weekly status report consolidating data from the divisions he supervised. His secretary called the division heads each week and obtained information from them which she then integrated manually into the standard report format. The v.p. asked IS whether this report could be speeded up with some kind of automated tool. IS responded quickly and determined that the information needed was available in several existing systems, and within a week wrote a program to consolidate the data and produce the report, reducing preparation time drastically. The secretary was given some simple instructions on how to kick the system off and the IS consultant left thinking he had won a major success. Weeks later the consultant noticed that the report was not being run, and called the v.p. to ask why. He replied that the system apparently didn't work as his secretary preferred to do things the old way. What had happened? The IS consultant neglected to take into account the concerns of the secretary, who not only spent a good portion of her week preparing this report, but in the process interacted with the heads of all the divisions! The new system threatened both her job security and her influence base in the organization, and she was positioned so that her refusal to use the system was enough to turn a smashing success into a flop. This is an extreme example of the impact of human factors on implementation, but the same concerns are present in every implementation. The consultant ignores them at his or her own risk.

Use the Consulting Cycle to Lay the Groundwork

This story illustrates another equally important lesson: successful implementation begins long before the implementation stage. Implementation concerns should be addressed during contracting and throughout the project. The Partner Map developed in the contracting stage should identify all affected groups and some methods for building support in those groups. Involving these groups in the consulting process is the best method—ensuring that they have input, directly or indirectly through a representative, to the direction the project takes. Before and during implementation, your job is to ensure there is adequate communication to these groups to keep them informed and to avoid surprises. You are asking for trouble if the building maintenance crew begins stringing cables over user's desks and they don't already:

- Understand the purpose and benefits of the new system.
- Understand what will be required of them and how it will affect their jobs.
- Feel that their concerns about the system have been identified and taken into account.
- Have an implementation and training schedule in their hands.
- Know who to call if they have questions about the project.

If you do not ensure a flow of accurate information about the project, the grapevine will fill the gaps, and the grapevine will probably base its assessment on past history with IS, rumors, and anxieties. The methods for predicting and managing client resistance in Chapter 13 are especially helpful in ensuring successful implementation.

Keep the Communication Lines Open

Work with the client to develop a communication strategy for these groups using the following steps:

1. Profile the audience(s) to be addressed. What are their key characteristics, goals, problems? What is their familiarity with technology?
2. List the aspects of the project that are likely to be seen favorably by the audience and the aspect they are likely to resist.
3. Based on this information, develop a communications strategy for building support for the project.

The strategy might include group meetings, memos, a project newsletter, individual communication between project team members and users, or a series of briefings down the area's management hierarchy, with managers and supervisors involved in briefing their people. Pick a method appropriate for the organization's culture and the characteristics of the audience. Whatever the strategy, make sure that client personnel play a major role so that the system is seen as their system.

STAGE 8—EVALUATION

Evaluation, like implementation, should be prepared for long before the stage begins.

Define Evaluation Criteria in the Contracting Stage

Asking the question "How will we know that this project is a success?" during your contracting meetings can be a remarkable tool for focusing the project effort, and the resulting criteria are not only the basis for evaluation, but a touchstone for testing whether the project effort is on track. If, halfway through the project, it becomes clear that the initial evaluation criteria no longer represent the goals of the project (as can happen when detailed data collection and analysis lead to rethinking the direction of the project), it is time to loop back to the contracting stage and reexamine the project's goals and parameters.

Encourage the Client to Take the Lead in Evaluating the Solution

This is especially important when evaluation involves gathering data from the users of the system; the effort should not be perceived as IS evaluating the users, but the users evaluating the effectiveness of the new system. Your role is to help the client:

- Clarify the evaluation criteria.
- Clarify their connections to business goals.
- Design an evaluation method.
- Compile and analyze results.

Building partnership at this stage of the cycle means ensuring that the evaluation is based on a sense of joint responsibility for the project. The evaluation results are a test of how well you did your job as well as an evaluation of the success of the system in solving business problems. Both you and the client should be open to learning from the evaluation process. Being open about what didn't work is often difficult given the time and effort that have been expended. It may be helpful to have an IS consultant and a client representative who were not directly involved in the project participate in the evaluation to gain added objectivity on the results.

One reason the consulting cycle is a cycle is that even after implementation the team will often surface problems and concerns that were not identified during the project. The results of the evaluation are not used simply to justify the project; they are input for the End/Extend stage.

Base the Evaluation on Business Criteria

The criteria selected for evaluation will vary depending on the client, the business problem, and the solution selected; but they should be focused on the client area's business goals and, wherever appropriate, the goals of the organization as a whole. Your job is to help the client move beyond generalities such as "we would like to automate this function" or "we would like to improve this function using a computer." On your side, avoid technical or usage-based justifications that have nothing to do with business success. That a system is in use 65 percent of the time, or has 300 log-ons per day, says little about the success or failure of the system in meeting business goals.

Use the Data Collection and Analysis Stage to Refine Evaluation Criteria

If the solution will be used by a large number of client personnel, it is wise to involve these people in setting the evaluation criteria. Do this by building into the data collection phase such questions as "what would this solution have to do in order for you to see it as a success?" The discussion following such open questions has other value in addition to building evaluation criteria. It reveals much about user expectations and can help the consultant and client to adjust the project to meet these expectations where they are on target, or to manage the expectations if they are unreasonable or outside the scope of the project.

Help the Client See the Solution in Broader Organizational Terms

With your organizationwide perspective and experience, you can also play a valuable role in helping the client see the project in terms of the overall organization's goals. How does this project link up with senior management's key concerns for the business? With specific objectives highlighted in the annual operating plan or strategic plan? If you know not only the organization but the business the organization is in, you can help the client look at the project in terms of its competitive impact. Do competing organizations have similar capabilities? Does the system build competitive advantage? Does it support the delivery of a new product, or shorten the delivery cycle, or help in differentiating a product offering from those of the competition? Does it help the organization deal with the impact of changes in the business environment, such as regulatory changes, entry of new competitors, changes in tax laws? Familiarity with the management literature on these and other aspects of the business can help you clarify for the client the importance of the project to the functional area and the business, as well as help to build support for the project.

Select Appropriate Evaluation Methods

How the evaluation is performed will depend on the criteria. The most clear-cut evaluations have quantifiable goals that can be measured by the system itself. For example, an order processing system might have the goal of reducing the average time from order to shipment to 24 hours. Given the proper inputs into the system, the system itself can produce audit reports that track the average time required.

Other systems will require some measurement by the users to provide data for evaluation. Measurement may involve interviews of users, using a questionnaire designed by the client and consultant, to determine their satisfaction and their opinion of the system's success in meeting the evaluation criteria. One of the best evaluation methods is interviewing the client organization's customers—whether internal or external. Who in other departments or in outside customer organizations uses the products of the system? Input from these areas is critical to assessing the full business impact of the project.

End-user systems such as personal computers, which may be used for a number of different tasks, are often evaluated on the basis of overall cost/benefit impact on the functional area. One way to perform this evaluation is to prepare in the contracting stage a chart that lists tasks that are planned for the new system, with estimates of hours per month spent on those tasks now, and expected hours per month using the new technology, giving a savings in hours per month. The hours saved can be multiplied by the hourly rate of the personnel using the system to indicate a dollar savings. (What figure to use for hourly rates is a question that should be addressed carefully to ensure that improper overheads are not applied that inflate the savings.)

After the system is installed, work with the client to gather data on actual usage and compare it to this initial estimate. This evaluation should be repeated again in six months, and again at one year after implementation to evaluate changes in usage. Of course, this analysis is limited, and cannot provide a complete picture of the value of the system. The follow-up evaluation should also include questions on additional value provided by the system such as cost avoidance, improved decision making, and new capabilities that are more qualitative. Figure 9–1 is an example of an evaluation form for general-use end-user systems.

Evaluate the Consulting Effort

Evaluation provides feedback on the effectiveness of your consulting effort. This feedback should be used within IS, in a postproject review. The purpose of this review is not fault-finding, but improvement—like the football team watching films of last week's game. The purpose is

FIGURE 9–1
Evaluation Form for End-User Systems

Client _____ Department/Mail Stop _____
System Requested _____
Total Cost _____ Monthly Cost (Total/60 months) _____

Prepurchase Cost/Savings Analysis

Task Performed	Current Hours/Mo	Estimated Hours/Mo	Savings Hours/Mo	User Salary $/Hr	Savings $/Mo
_____	_____ −	_____ =	_____ *	_____ =	_____
_____	_____ −	_____ =	_____ *	_____ =	_____
_____	_____ −	_____ =	_____ *	_____ =	_____
_____	_____ −	_____ =	_____ *	_____ =	_____
_____	_____ −	_____ =	_____ *	_____ =	_____
_____	_____ −	_____ =	_____ *	_____ =	_____
_____	_____ −	_____ =	_____ *	_____ =	_____
_____	_____ −	_____ =	_____ *	_____ =	_____

Total Estimated Monthly Savings   _____

6-Month Evaluation

Task Performed	Previous Hours/Mo	Actual Hours/Mo	Savings Hours/Mo	User Salary $/Hr	Savings $/Mo
_____	_____ −	_____ =	_____ *	_____ =	_____
_____	_____ −	_____ =	_____ *	_____ =	_____
_____	_____ −	_____ =	_____ *	_____ =	_____
_____	_____ −	_____ =	_____ *	_____ =	_____
_____	_____ −	_____ =	_____ *	_____ =	_____
_____	_____ −	_____ =	_____ *	_____ =	_____
_____	_____ −	_____ =	_____ *	_____ =	_____
_____	_____ −	_____ =	_____ *	_____ =	_____

Total Actual Monthly Savings   _____

Are you using the system to perform any additional tasks that were not performed previously? If so, describe these tasks and the business benefit of performing them.

_____

_____

_____

_____

not to cause pain for anyone who made mistakes (though it is a rare project where a clear look back will not cause some wincing), but to see the mistakes clearly so they can be avoided next time. This evaluation data is a gold mine of learning for the consulting team. The press of new requests and the natural tendency to put the old project to bed and move on have to be resisted in order to take advantage of the opportunity for growth that evaluation presents.

Use Evaluation Data to Make the Business Case for IS

Evaluation provides solid evidence for payoff from the organization's technology investment. Individually, it will build confidence and support with specific clients and is an important part of their education in how to evaluate the need for future projects. Across the board, it provides IS with the data that is necessary to respond to the more and more frequent requests from senior management for a hard-nosed assessment of the IS organization's role. Inability to answer this question to management's satisfaction is one factor in IS's frequent lack of credibility. And building the data collection needed to answer this question into each and every project makes answering much easier.

STAGE 9—END OR EXTEND

Use Evaluation Data to Determine Next Steps

Data from the evaluation stage is the basis for the End/Extend project stage, where you and the client assess the success and shortcomings of the solution and determine whether additional effort is required. Discuss this data with the client at a project review meeting. If the project has clarified additional needs, or clarified the original need in such a way that additional work is required, then a decision may be made to extend the project. At this point the consulting cycle must begin again. This may require a new "request for services" if that is part of the organization's procedures, along with an evaluation of other priorities to determine when the work can be scheduled. It will definitely require recontracting. It may make sense for a different consultant to handle the extended project. The client and consultant roles may be redefined based on the results of the first project or the requirements of the extension. The important point for you is to ensure that the client understands that the additional effort is a new project.

If the client is satisfied with the results, this is the end of the project. With partnership successfully established, however, it should not be the end of communication with the client. At a minimum, a commitment to reevaluate the solution in six months should be firmed up. But the value of partnership extends beyond the end of the project. The client has been educated in the project process as well as in the technology. You have been given a course in the workings of the client's area. This cross-fertilization adds value on both sides. The client may now serve as a resource to IS on future projects. And the client can now use you, and IS in general, as a higher-level resource on future projects.

PART 3

THE PARTNERSHIP TOOLBOX: TECHNIQUES FOR MANAGING THE HUMAN SIDE

CHAPTER 10

STRUCTURING THE HUMAN SIDE OF IS PROJECTS: THE PARTNER MAP

One way to ensure that the organizational side of a project is covered as adequately as the technical side is to set aside some time at the beginning of the project to profile the potential partners for the project: the key people in the organization who could have an impact, positive or negative, on the success of the project. The partner map at the end of this chapter is designed to give structure to this analysis. It provides a form for identifying five types of partners as well as potential resisters or roadblocks.

PROBLEM-SOLVING PARTNER

This is your primary client. This may seem obvious, but there are instances where it is not. It is always a valuable exercise to ask the question, "Who is the client?" Perhaps the project is being requested by one manager but driven by another. Perhaps one manager delegated joint responsibility for the project to two subordinates. In such cases it may be unclear who the primary client actually is. It may be necessary to work with more than one client, but be aware that to do so complicates the important task of building partnership.

INFORMATION PARTNERS

This category includes the various people you need information from to make the project work. Identifying these people up front helps ensure that they do not fall through the cracks as the project proceeds. Information partners may also be people you need to keep informed about the project, whether to get feedback about the impact of project activities on other aspects of the business, or simply to keep the person from feeling left out, threatened, or insecure. Keeping people on the periphery of the project informed can defuse potential conflicts that could derail the project.

LOBBYING PARTNERS

These are key people who will not be directly involved in the project, but who are favorably disposed to it and can use their influence to push the project forward. Such allies are a valuable asset and should be identified and cultivated. A lobbying partner might be a supporter in a group which is otherwise resistant to the project, who can help swing the group to a more favorable position. Or a manager who will be present in a key review meeting on the project, who with some careful preselling will voice her support to senior management.

SPONSORING PARTNERS

This category includes high-level managers who are championing the project and are willing and able to use their authority to make the project happen. A sponsoring partner can make resources available, delegate project tasks to subordinates, rearrange priorities to speed progress on the project, and minimize resistance. Of course, such a resource must be used carefully; they usually have a wide range of priorities and a busy schedule. A sponsoring partner is especially important when a project involves significant change across more than one functional area or department.

AFFECTED GROUPS

These are groups that will feel the impact of the project. Identify all these groups during the contracting phase, because they will influence the success of the project. Whose procedures will change as a result of the project? Whose job responsibilities or interfaces with other groups will change? Who will use outputs of the new system as inputs into their processes? IS projects, even small ones, can have wide-ranging impacts in an organization. Managing that impact is part of your job.

Even change that affects someone positively, if it is preceded by lack of involvement and lack of communication with the agents of the change, can lead to resistance. And the smallness or apparent triviality of the change should not be seen as an excuse to leave a group uninvolved and uninformed. Something as simple as replacing a terminal with the vendor's newest replacement model with exactly the same functionality can cause anxiety or confusion that can negatively impact the project. If those affected are brought into the loop up front, where adjustments can be made more easily, major disruptions can be avoided later on in the project. Once the affected groups are identified, you can work to minimize the disruptive effects of change, communicate the benefits, openly address people's concerns, and build support for the project among those who will be affected. The most common mistake is simply not taking the time to identify all these people.

ROADBLOCKS

In addition to supportive partners and affected groups, identify potential sources of resistance to the project. Who may perceive the project as threatening their power base or job security? Who may feel uncomfortable with the technology and mask their discomfort with criticism of the system? Roadblocks may include a key user who is comfortable with the status quo and resistant to change in general, an administrator who has concerns about losing control when the new solution is implemented because his two younger assistants are more familiar with computers, or a manager who has another use in mind for the money budgeted for the project. Identifying these potential problems early gives you an edge in developing ways to manage them or at least buffer the project from their negative effects. Putting the roadblocks on the same sheet with the partners helps generate creative ideas about employing these partners in minimizing resistance.

The Partner Map (Figure 10–1) lays out a political or organizational guide to the project. It also opens the project up, giving a broader view of the task and its ramifications in the larger environment. This broader view often has a real benefit: it enables you to get "out of the

FIGURE 10–1
Partner Map

Problem-Solving Partner: _____

Partner you work with directly.
May represent a group or a higher-level client.
Decision maker, accountable for project success.

Information Partners:

Those you need information from:

_____   _____
_____   _____
_____   _____
_____

Usually not decision makers.
Provide data on project or environment.

Those you need to keep informed:

_____   _____
_____

Part of resource network.
Usually not directly involved in project.
Can have impact on project.
Should not be surprised by project developments.

Lobbying Partners:

_____   _____

Can speak up for project at key junctions with key audiences.
May be part of client or consultant organization.
Usually need to be sold on benefits to them.

Sponsor Partners:

_____   _____

Influential, opinion shapers.
Can open doors and free up resources.
Have significant stake in successful implementation.

Affected Groups:

_____   _____
_____   _____
_____   _____

Jobs, procedures, interfaces will change as a result of project.
Can impact project momentum if not supportive.

FIGURE 10–1—*Concluded*

> **Roadblocks:**
>
> ————————————— ——————————————
> ————————————— ——————————————
>
> Likely to resist or object to project.
> Can be individuals, groups, cultural forces.

box" and see all sorts of creative ways to make the project work that are not visible when maintaining a narrow focus on the problem at hand. Most IS professionals have the skills and aptitude to sketch the political lay of the land in this way, but all too often this aspect of the project gets no attention. The partner map, built into a consulting methodology, can make it a habit. A good way to use this tool is to share it with the client; or if the chemistry is right, develop it in partnership with the client. The client will probably be able to correct some misconceptions on your map and add some partners to the list. Talking about the map may also help clarify the organizational impact of the project for the client and lead to fruitful changes in the contracting process and the project plan.

CHAPTER 11

PARTNERSHIP IN PROCESS: INTERACTIVE LISTENING

Take a minute and—using your whole life as the database—think of three people you know whom you consider to be excellent listeners. Having trouble coming up with three names? Most people do when asked this question. There is a real lesson here—excellent listening is a rare skill. Now, thinking about the names you did come up with, are any of these excellent listeners people you do not like and respect? The lesson is powerful and clear: being a good listener is almost unequalled as a means of building goodwill and respect with your clients.

Because listening is such an important skill for building partnership, we have developed a technique called interactive listening, built around a four-stage process we call the H.E.A.R. model. This technique can and should be employed in all consultant/client communication. As is evident from the letters and phone calls we get from people with whom we have shared this model, it even works with staff members, bosses, spouses, and children.

We call the technique interactive listening because it is two-way communication, with the emphasis on building the consultant/client partnership. The H.E.A.R. model divides the listening process into four steps:

1. Hear
2. Empathize
3. Analyze
4. Respond

These four steps may be repeated once in a quick phone call, or fifty times in a project meeting.

STEP 1—HEAR

The first step in interactive listening is to actually hear what is being said. The listener must give the speaker full attention. If you think back to a less-than-exciting lecture you attended you will probably recall tuning the speaker in and out. The same thing often happens in meetings and conversation; we only hear a portion of what is said. It takes real effort to focus for extended periods on what someone is saying. So first and foremost, interactive listening requires concentration—you must make a mental commitment to focus your attention on what your client is saying.

Hearing what is said also requires that the listener eliminate both external and internal noise. External noise includes the phone calls, the interruptions by visitors, the traffic sound on the street outside, the construction workers on the floor above, the noisy impact printer outside the door. Noise can be visual as well as aural: people walking by an open door, the window cleaners perched on their scaffolding across the street. Minimize external activity that distracts attention from the speaker when selecting a setting for the client meeting. Of course, noise can never be eliminated entirely, and at times it may be necessary to meet in less than favorable conditions. For this reason you must also develop the discipline to deliberately tune out the noise and focus on what is being said.

Internal noise can be even more dangerous than the external variety. Internal noise includes all the other issues on your mind, the argument you had with your boss this morning, the seven other projects on your to-do list, your next meeting, the laundry that has to be picked up after work. Some people claim that because thinking is faster than speech, they can think about other issues while listening. We find that this does not work. Every time your mind wanders to one of these other subjects you are tuning the client out. Not only are you missing important information, but the client more often than not will sense the lack of attention. Instead of wandering to other issues, plow your leftover thinking time right into the listening process, noting the client's nonverbal communication (tone, body language, energy level), summarizing key points, taking a few quick notes.

One of the most dangerous forms of internal noise is mental arguing. How often do we begin to disagree mentally even before the other person has said three sentences? There is no better way to make sure that a client does not share information fully than to engage in this mental arguing. People are surprisingly perceptive of a listener's mental attitudes; they are reflected in facial expressions and body language in ways that are difficult if not impossible to control.

Each step in the H.E.A.R. model, including this first step, is interactive. Periodically feed back what you have heard to the client to check your accuracy and let your client know that you understand. Do so by summarizing key points in your own words, and asking the client for verification. "Let me make sure I understood the last three issues you brought up. Is that accurate?" This feedback loop is what makes listening a partnership-building process.

STEP 2—EMPATHIZE

Once you have heard the client, the second step in the interactive listening process is to empathize, to see from the client's perspective and understand how he or she *feels* about the issue being discussed. When we say that someone is a good listener, we usually mean that we feel understood by that person. We instinctively sense the presence of empathy.

It is important to distinguish between empathy and sympathy. It is not necessary to sympathize with the client (to agree with the client's point of view and feel the same way he or she does); in practice, there will be times when you will and times when you won't. You can empathize whether or not you feel sympathy. Empathy means understanding what a client feels and why—glimpsing the underlying reasons for the feelings. To do this effectively, you must:

• Show your interest in understanding the client's point of view if your own is different.
• Listen for feelings and ideas as well as facts.
• Listen for the "music behind the words"—the context in which the client is working.
• Respect the client's position.

How can you empathize? After hearing the client present a problem, put yourself in the client's place and think about what it would be like to be in the client's position. How would you feel? What factors would influence your perception?

This stage is also a two-way process. In addition to feeding back the facts you have heard, paraphrase and summarize the client's position in order to check for accuracy and show the client that you understand. Empathy is the sine qua non of good listening. It builds trust, because the client sees that you really understand what it's like to live where he or she lives. It encourages the client to provide more information, because it is clear that he or she is actually being listened to. Perhaps the most important thing empathy does is build confidence in your analysis. Without showing the client empathy, you can have the most logical, cost-justified, politically astute, surefire analysis in the world, and the client can discount it, because you "don't know what it's like to . . . ". If you have listened with empathy, and communicated that empathy back to the client, the client must take your analysis seriously, even if he or she disagrees with it, because it is based on a clear understanding of the client's position.

STEP 3—ANALYZE

Most IS professionals don't need any help with this stage. Analysis is part of their training, and they can do it in their sleep. What they do need practice with is holding off on analysis long enough to hear what the client is saying and to empathize. Many of us begin to analyze as soon as someone begins to speak. This is as much a form of internal noise as thinking about the movie you saw last night.

Premature analysis causes two problems. First, the analysis will probably be wrong, because you haven't taken the time to get the facts. Second, it will usually alienate the client, who may feel that you are glossing over whole aspects of the problem. This in turn will lead to a loss of confidence in your ability to get things done in his or her environment. The client may even feel that you have trivialized the problem.

Once empathy has been achieved, however, you need to apply all your analytical skills to the data the client provides. Use open-ended questions to help the client explore the situation and put a broad range of facts and reactions on the table. Use directive, probing questions to zero in on areas where an in-depth understanding is critical to your analysis.

To make this step interactive, you must walk the client through your analysis, building a shared understanding of the situation. Make explicit which inferences you drew from which facts, ideas, and feelings presented by the client. And don't assume that the client agrees with your analysis. Ask for feedback on what does and doesn't fit from the client's viewpoint. You want the result to be "our" analysis, not "my" analysis. This is the foundation for client commitment to your recommendations.

STEP 4—RESPOND

The final stage of interactive listening is to respond. One brand of poor listeners uses the one-stage "R" model: they respond immediately, without hearing, empathizing, or analyzing. This "name that tune" style may save time, but it is usually not very effective. Yet responding is a necessary part of the two-way communication involved in effective listening. Picture yourself as a client in an interview with a consultant. You have patiently answered all his questions for two hours, and all he has done is take notes and go on to ask the next question. You are likely to feel threatened, angry, or both; you have worked hard and gotten nothing in return.

Your responses in the listening process are an opportunity to give the client value. That value can include understanding, encouragement, clarification, a sense of progress, a clear sense of direction on the project. Each little bit of value the consultant adds encourages the client to provide more information, while building a real atmosphere of partnership.

Your response is much more likely to have maximum value if it is based on accurate hearing, empathy, and shared analysis. If it is, it should not surprise the client. Make sure you respond in language the client will understand. This means avoiding jargon and making sure that the response is clearly framed in terms of the problem being discussed. Connect your response explicitly to previous areas of mutual analysis and agreement. And if the response includes recommendations for action, be specific about who needs to do what and when as a result of your analysis.

To close the feedback loop on this final stage, check to make sure the client understands your response as you intended it. Ask the client to paraphrase your response, and test for both understanding and comfort level.

SUMMARY

Here is a quick summary of the H.E.A.R. model. It can be useful as a review before you go into a client meeting, or as an outline to be used in the meeting itself.

1. HEAR

   Make a mental commitment to listen.
   Eliminate internal/external noise.
   Periodically feed back what you have heard to test for accuracy.

2. EMPATHIZE

   Work to understand and respect the client's point of view even if yours is different.
   Listen for feelings/ideas.
   Paraphrase the client's position to test for accuracy.

3. ANALYZE

   Hold off on analysis until you have finished stage 2.
   Walk the client through your analytical framework to build a *shared* analysis.
   Ask for feedback on what fits and what doesn't.

4. RESPOND

   Use your response to add value.
   Respond in language the client will understand.
   Connect your response to previous areas of mutual agreement.
   Be specific about needed actions.
   Ask the client to paraphrase your response and comment on it.

CHAPTER 12

STRUCTURING CLIENT MEETINGS FOR SUCCESS

One of the most common complaints from IS professionals is an inability to get their clients' time. They can't get on their client's calendar, the client's other priorities take precedence over project meetings, the client cancels appointments at the last minute. This problem has many roots, but at bottom, clients do what they perceive will give them the most return on their time investment. One sure way to *create* a problem getting client time is to waste that time once you get it. Yet how often do we give clients real value for time spent in project meetings? And how often do we leave them feeling frustrated?

Think of a particularly frustrating meeting you have attended. What was wrong with it? Perhaps one person took over and focused on one relatively unimportant issue. Or it meandered off track, leaving the participants feeling the agony of a wasted morning. Or it ended with a feeling that nothing was accomplished, with no one really sure what was to happen next. The problem in such failed meetings is usually a lack of structure, compounded by a lack of effective facilitative control. Structuring your meetings into the following five steps addresses both problems: (1) prepare; (2) open; (3) conduct; (4) close; (5) follow up.

Meetings that fail often use the one-step model: conduct. Handling the "meat" of the meeting is a task in itself, but it is the two steps on either side of "conduct" that often separate the good meetings from the bad.

STEP 1—PREPARING FOR THE MEETING

There is no substitute for doing your homework. The care taken in preparing will increase your control over the meeting. In addition, the time spent will be apparent to the client and will reinforce the partnership relationship.

Define Your Objectives

What do you really want to achieve in the meeting? This may seem like an obvious question, but spending five minutes thinking about it can clarify the issue and save valuable time during the meeting. Too often, IS consultants go into a data collection meeting looking for too much information, or looking for information from the wrong source. Usually the cause is a lack of time to think through the objectives before the meeting. Make room in your schedule to jot down objectives and then refine them. If you are unclear about the objectives, perhaps the meeting isn't necessary, or perhaps it should be delayed until more information is gathered.

Prepare an Agenda

Once the objectives are clarified, preparing an agenda is much easier. Since you will share this agenda with the client before the meeting and use it during the meeting, you should pay some attention to the wording of the key points, making sure they are clear and not misleading, that they are action oriented, and that their pertinence to the project will be clear to the client.

Include the objectives and the key items in the closing on the agenda. This prepares others in the meeting for the way you will conduct it and eliminates surprise. It also helps keep things on track and reduces the chance that someone will leave before the closing.

Prepare Key Questions

Formulating specific questions gives you an edge going into the meeting. Of course, you can't predict all areas to be covered, and any list of questions prepared in advance will inevitably include some questions that will never be asked. Still, there are good reasons for preparing the list in advance. Like the agenda, it helps to improve control over the meeting. It will build your confidence and the client's trust. And the process of thinking through the questions often helps clarify the problem itself.

Make Sure the Relevance of Questions Is Obvious

When preparing questions, test them against the objectives of the meeting to ensure that each one clearly relates to at least one of those objectives. The relevance and importance of each question should be obvious to the client, otherwise the question might undermine client trust. If the objective of a question is not self-evident, try rewording it. If necessary, place the question in context using a lead-in explanation.

Don't Include Questions that
Produce Data You Can't Handle

Think about how the client will answer the question. Will the question produce information in a form you can handle? Or do you need to do some homework before you can process the answer? Don't waste the client's time covering issues you are not ready for. As with the objectives and agenda, reviewing the questions with other members of the IS project team is helpful.

In most cases, the questions you prepare beforehand will be open ended rather than closed. Closed questions ask for a yes or no or other limited answer; open questions encourage the client to discuss the issue at some length, and provide you with the understanding of the context of the problem, the client's feelings and ideas about the problem, and other issues that the client feels are important. Table 12–1 shows some examples of closed and open questions for typical IS consulting situations.

Leading off with closed questions can prevent valuable background or context information from coming to light. However, closed questions should be used later in the meeting to focus in on a specific area once discussion has been initiated. They are useful for clarifying ambiguities, double-checking on details, verifying facts. Some examples are shown in Table 12–2.

One question to avoid assiduously in client meetings is "Why?" This three-letter word is dangerous and can make the client feel his or her judgment is being questioned. IS professionals need to be especially

TABLE 12–1
Examples of Closed and Open Questions

Situation	Closed Question	Open Question
Discussion of new human resource system	Does your current system handle salary, employee records, and performance data?	What functions does your current HR system perform?
Discussion of printer problem	Does this problem occur frequently?	Tell me about the problem—how often and under what circumstances does it occur?
Discussion of new electronic mail capability	You've seen the new EMAIL system: does it meet your needs?	How does the new EMAIL system look in relation to your needs?

sensitive to such questions, because in our role as change agents and introducers of technology we have a history of changing (and sometimes eliminating) jobs. In nearly every case the same information can be obtained using different, nonthreatening words as in Table 12–3.

Pay Attention to the Time and Setting

Spend a few minutes thinking about where and when the meeting will be held. How will the place and time affect the meeting? How long will

TABLE 12–2
Effective Closed Questions

Situation	Effective Closed Question
Verifying problem with existing system	Do I understand correctly that the key problem is slow response time on queries, which wastes time in customer service telephone calls?
Clarifying ambiguity in description	I'm unclear; was the requisition or the purchase order the source of that data item?

TABLE 12–3
Alternatives to "Why" Questions

"Why" Question	Alternative Nonthreatening Question
Why did you decide on that software?	What features attracted you to that software?
Why did that data entry method fail?	What problems did you experience with that data entry method?
Why haven't you used the existing system more effectively?	What factors have kept you from getting real benefit from the existing system?

the meeting take? Should it be broken into two sessions? Your goal is to minimize interruptions and other problems that will decrease the effectiveness of the meeting and to ensure that the atmosphere will increase the client's comfort and motivation. If the meeting will be held in the client's office, how will interruptions be controlled? If it will be held in your office, will the client feel less comfortable and perhaps less open? If the meeting is to be held on Friday before a holiday weekend, is the client planning to leave early, so that he or she might be less motivated to contribute actively? Most of the considerations here are common sense. The key is to pay attention to them so that common sense gets a chance to work.

If several client personnel will attend the meeting, must they all stay for the entire meeting? Or can the meeting be structured so that one or more people attend only part of it? Your ability to save clients time in meetings will strengthen your influence with those clients. They will be more likely to come to your next meeting if they know you won't waste their time.

STEP 2—OPENING THE MEETING

The opening sets the tone for the meeting and lays the foundation for working together. You have four goals in the opening:

1. Reduce anxiety.
2. Review objectives.

3. Review agenda.
4. Review roles.

Take a quick scan of the attendees before starting and think about how to create a productive atmosphere for the meeting. The client may have had a lousy morning. She may be feeling real concern about the project and be in a negative frame of mind. Your job is to spread your confidence and enthusiasm to the client and begin things on a positive note.

The remainder of the opening puts the meeting on course immediately by reviewing objectives, agenda, and roles. Even if the agenda and objectives were reviewed with the client in advance, test them for clarity and agreement again during the opening and be open to modifications by the client. Briefly reviewing your role as facilitator, and the roles of the other people in the meeting, also sets the stage for success. This is especially important if some of the attendees do not know each other or do not understand what part someone in the room is playing in the project. Making needed introductions and clarifying who is there to do what reduces anxiety and helps focus the meeting.

STEP 3—CONDUCTING THE MEETING

During the body of the meeting, your goal is to obtain the most useful information from the client, build client trust and motivation, and build project momentum. Sticking close to the following rules will support these goals.

Make Sure the Meeting Is Productive

It is a rare client that objects when the consultant takes charge of the process in order to get the work done in the time allotted. As facilitator for the meeting you take responsibility for controlling the flow of the data collection process, making sure that all points of view are heard, and that the discussion doesn't wander off track. Keep an eye on the clock and work the agenda. Of course, you must stay flexible and be willing to allot more time to one agenda item or add additional items based on what happens in the meeting. But in such cases you should do so explicitly, clarify for the others in the meeting the ramifications of those actions, and get their agreement. For example, you might say: "It looks like the interface with the purchasing department is a key issue here; this wasn't on our agenda, but we can either address it now and put off one of today's topics, or hold off on it until next time."

Turn Information into Solvable Problems

Seize the opportunity to act as a consultant on the spot by packaging information provided by the client into solvable problems. You may need to turn blameful statements, generalities, vague negative judgments, and other counterproductive language into problems that are addressable through actions by you or other members of the team. In the course of the meeting build a list of these solvable problems, stated in manageable terms, that can be fed back to the client for review and clarification. From that list identify next steps, action commitments, and open or unresolved issues. These will be restated to the attendees during the closing.

Clarify Project Roles

During data collection meetings, take advantage of opportunities to clarify the client's role and your role in the project. For example, if you are part of an End-User Computing Support group whose charter is to provide problem clarification, support, and training, with the user responsible for setting goals, selecting among solution options, and implementing the solution, your questions and responses to the client should make these ground rules clear. The way you work on the problem with the client should clearly reflect these roles.

Be Yourself

Be genuine, and don't hide in a professional shell. A sense of humor, a talent for making people feel comfortable, a natural enthusiasm, a winning smile, are all valuable tools in consulting. Each of us has personal strengths, and the key to use them appropriately. Trust your instincts and intuitions, and don't be afraid to be authentic in sharing judgments, reactions, and concerns with the client. This openness builds trust and helps to ensure success.

STEP 4—CLOSING THE MEETING

How many client meetings end with one or more people running out the door, frantic to get to their next appointment? How many end with the attendees looking at their watches after the person running the meeting has asked them to stay "just a few minutes longer?" Building a closing into the agenda can solve these problems and foster client goodwill. Unless everyone in the meeting is clearly motivated to continue past the schedule ending time, it is your duty as the facilitator to call a halt 5 to 10 minutes before the end and close the meeting properly. This is much easier to accomplish if you include the four closing steps on the agenda in the first place:

1. Review and summary.
2. Next steps.
3. Action commitments.
4. Meeting analysis.

In that final 5 or 10 minutes, review what has been covered in the meeting. Walk through the agenda points and highlight what was accomplished on each. Review the list of next steps you have collected during the meeting and firm up the action commitments based on these next steps. It is important to include accountabilities and completion dates for these actions. If action commitments are made for people not present at the meeting, make briefing those people and getting them on board an additional action commitment.

As you review these items, test for agreement on the part of the client and any other participants, watching for verbal or nonverbal clues that someone is uncomfortable with the summary. Such clues can indicate misunderstanding or resistance that has not been brought to the surface. In either case this discomfort should be acknowledged and clarified, and not swept under the rug. If time is too short, acknowledge the open issue and schedule a follow-up meeting to resolve it.

The final agenda point is an analysis of the meeting. This does not mean a blow-by-blow discussion, but a brief "How did we do?" A good way to introduce this topic is to simply ask the question "Do you feel that this meeting was productive?" Solicit suggestions on how to improve things for the next meeting. Perhaps the time or the setting can be changed to reduce interruptions. Perhaps other people should be invited to provide additional input. This brief analysis gives such ideas a chance to surface and also shows the client that you are interested in improving and adapting to meet the client's needs.

STEP 5—FOLLOW UP

You know what it's like to walk out of an IS project meeting and into the midst of a dozen other priority issues. That two hours of confidence building, data gathering, negotiating, and note taking all too often gets thrown into a desk drawer to be ignored for hours or even days. Client confidence plummets when the client finds that a week has passed since the meeting and no progress has been made. And the client will be much less likely to be enthusiastic about the next two-hour meeting. Two simple rules prevent this from happening.

Work with the Data Immediately

Most people take notes in a form of personal shorthand. This is almost a necessity in the meeting process: there are few better ways to lose someone's enthusiasm and attention than to copy down everything the person says. Some people have trouble deciphering their own shorthand if they wait more than an hour or two after the meeting. The information garnered from the interaction is stored in short-term memory, and that information fades quickly, especially when other demands are made on the brain immediately. The best way to protect this valuable data is to work with it as soon as the meeting is over, finishing incomplete sentences, circling and underlining key points, drawing arrows to connect related thoughts, whatever you need to do to put the data into a form that will be usable later on.

Unless you are more disciplined than most people, you will seldom do this follow-up analysis unless you build it into your schedule in the first place. This means that a 45-minute meeting goes on your calendar as 60 minutes. If the meeting is in a conference room, schedule the room for that additional 15 minutes, and stay after the other attendees have left. If the meeting is in the client's office, or in your office where interruptions will demand your attention, sneak out to a quiet place— the company library, or the cafeteria outside of meal hours, to do the wrap up. This time can also be used to add action commitments to your calendar, and to make a personal to-do list in order to carry those actions out successfully. Once this has been done, you can address your dozen other pressing commitments with more clarity and confidence.

Communicate Frequently with the Client

Keep the client in the loop. Remember that the work relationship with the client is one of the three legs of any project. If the client doesn't know what's going on with the project, all sorts of unfortunate things happen. The client may:

- Lose enthusiasm for the project and give it a lower priority because progress is not visible.
- Lose confidence in your ability to make things happen.
- Be embarrassed by a question or comment on the project from someone else who is more informed.

Sean, an IS systems analyst with expertise in rapid system development, was leading a project team on a two-month, high-priority development project for a marketing manager. The project was ahead of schedule. Basic data collection had been completed, and the team was working full speed ahead on a prototype to present to the client. Two weeks had gone by, and the prototype was almost ready. Sean wanted to be able to surprise the client and deliver the prototype at the next client meeting and held off contacting the client until work on the prototype was completed. The client met with the CEO on another issue and made an offhand comment that the project Sean was leading didn't seem to be going anywhere. Even if Sean found out about such a comment, undoing the damage and erasing the black mark next to his name in the CEO's mind would be difficult.

Breaking the stream of client communication is so easy, especially when the project is only one item on your crowded agenda. The more projects, the more important ongoing communication becomes, yet the more difficult it is to find the time to do it. For IS professionals who are focused on the technical issues, client communication often gets short shrift when schedules are overloaded.

The solution? Build client contact into your weekly schedule. Block out one half-hour slot a week. In many cases all that will be needed is a two-minute phone call that updates the client on project progress and gives the client a chance to ask questions or voice concerns. These two-minute calls have a tremendous payoff in client confidence and in keeping the project on track in a changing environment.

Another useful method for keeping in touch with clients is the "just happened to be in the neighborhood" visit. One internal consultant we know uses what he calls the "golden time" around 5:15 in the evening, when many workers have already left for the day, to drop in on clients with a quick update and some tidbits of information the consultant knows will be appreciated. This consultant knows there will be times when the client is too busy to talk, and in such cases takes the appropriate and courteous course—perhaps limiting his visit to a minute or

TABLE 12–4
Meeting Checklist

1. Prepare.
   a. Define your objectives.
   b. Prepare an agenda.
   c. Communicate the agenda in advance.
   d. Prepare key questions.
   e. Make sure the relevance of questions is obvious.
   f. Don't include questions that produce data you can't handle.
   g. Pay attention to time and setting.
2. Open.
   a. Reduce anxiety.
   b. Review objectives.
   c. Review agenda.
   d. Review roles.
3. Conduct.
   a. Make sure the meeting is productive.
   b. Turn information into solvable problems.
   c. Clarify project roles.
   d. Be yourself.
   e. Use interactive listening.
   f. Provide immediate benefit to the client.
4. Close.
   a. Review and summarize.
   b. Next step.
   c. Action commitments.
   d. Analysis of meeting.
5. Follow up.
   a. Work with the data as soon as possible.
   b. Communicate frequently with the client.

dropping off a written progress report. Then there are times when these impromptu meetings can turn into half-hour conversations that provide a gold mine of information and insight. With the pressure off, in the informality of an after-hours visit, the client will often feel more comfortable sharing goals, gripes, and the broader perspective of his or her position.

The meeting checklist (see Table 12–4), summarizes the five steps in a successful meeting and the key tasks in each step. Tape a copy on your project notepad and check off the steps as they are completed.

CHAPTER 13

PREDICTING AND MANAGING CLIENT RESISTANCE

Frank, a manager of internal communications for a large but conservative insurance firm, had been with the company for 30 years and had advanced from the position of courier in the mail room to managing the internal mail operation, the word processing pool, and the production of internal newsletters. He received a management edict to automate and streamline the internal mail system, and to double the frequency of the four newsletters his group produced from bimonthly to monthly. His familiarity with technology extended only to the standalone word processing units his pool used to produce documents.

When he came to IS for help with his problem, Frank stressed his group's success in doing the jobs assigned to them. The word processing pool had gotten a terrific return on the investment in the systems and had a good record of on-time delivery. The two people on his staff who produced the newletters often had to work nights and weekends, but they got the newsletters out on time. And as far as he knew, no one had ever complained about his internal mail operation losing a message. He was obviously proud of the job he had done.

Sue, the IS analyst, worked to build rapport with Frank and get things off to a solid start. They worked out a project plan and set up a first data collection meeting. At this meeting, Sue began to ask questions about the current procedures, but Frank kept getting off the track. He returned again and again to the good job his group had done and to his frustration with the management edict. He showed little interest in focusing on how to solve the problem at hand, and even implied that he didn't see how the effort could be successful.

For many IS professionals, dealing with client resistance like this is one of the most difficult parts of their job. Identifying and coping with resistance requires intuition, tact, patience, and constant attention to all aspects of the client's communication regarding the project. It also helps to have a technique for dealing with resistance in a creative way.

WHAT IS RESISTANCE?

The first step in dealing with resistance is understanding that it is:

- A natural and predictable response to change.
- A sign that you are working on significant issues.
- Usually indirectly expressed by the client.

Your first goal in dealing with resistance is to *predict and manage* it before it becomes a problem. Resistance is a predictable response to any change that will affect how the work is going to get done, how jobs are defined, how information will be communicated, and how results will be measured. Your job is to be a change agent, to facilitate the process of change; this includes seeing where resistance is likely to occur and working out strategies to address it. The following list of questions can help you clarify areas of potential resistance and develop strategies to manage it.

1. Do the client and other affected groups see a need to change the status quo? Has management identified the limitations of the status quo in relation to current or near future business conditions? Some frustration with the status quo must exist (or be generated) before the client will be motivated to see the change through.

What you can do: Profile the groups that do not see the need for change. Help management clarify and communicate the problems with the status quo in terms that these groups will respond to. Or help management generate (e.g., through incorporation into performance objectives) motivation to change.

2. Do those who will be affected by the change have an opportunity to give significant input on the project, beginning in the planning stages? People tend to support change when they have had some involvement in shaping it. When they are given this opportunity, potential concerns can surface early, and the reasons for changing the status quo can be explained. Without this involvement, those affected by the change will feel disenfranchised and controlled, rather than empowered by the project, planting seeds for later resistance.

What you can do: Construct a partner map (see Chapter 10) identifying all affected groups. Profile these groups and build opportunities for input from each of these groups into the project as early as possible.

3. Does the investment/payback ratio make good business sense to the client? Have all costs (not just dollars) been recognized, and does the expected payback clearly outweigh the cost in the client's perception? In the perception of others affected by the change?

What you can do: Work with client management to build a thorough and realistic picture of the costs and payback. Test for clear commitment to the change based on this information in all affected areas. Help clients exploit the benefits.

4. Do those affected (top, middle, and first-line management as well as individual contributors) understand the change process itself? Ignorance of the process can lead to resistance.

What you can do: Use the consulting cycle to:

a. Outline the stages of the process in order to minimize false expectations.

b. Clarify the commitments required of all parties.

c. Help those affected understand the uncertainties, impacts, and consequences of the change.

d. Create a climate in which all involved with the project are encouraged to identify and address potential problems along the way instead of covering them up or assuming that it is someone else's job to take care of them.

5. Are key people in the client organization *perceived* to be in support of the change? Perception is the key word here. If the movers and shakers in the organization are behind the project effort, but only when behind closed doors, there will be problems. Their support must be visible and continuing to be effective in minimizing resistance. In addition, this support must be consistent throughout the chain of command. Most people monitor their own boss most carefully. A project that has highly visible top management support will still be resisted if first-line supervisors are perceived as being skeptical or reluctant to support the change.

What you can do: Build and maintain a model of project support to use as a guide:

a. Map areas of support and resistance throughout the change process.

b. Work to understand and address resisters' concerns.

c. Help supporters understand the ways in which they can express their support (including influencing resisters).

d. Assist client management in providing appropriate reward structures (praise, recognition, increased authority and control, financial benefits, increased job satisfaction) for those supporting the change.

6. What partnership relationship exists between the client organization and IS? What is IS's track record with this client? The greater the change, the more the project requires a solid partnership relationship, with both parties committed and working together.

What you can do: Educate the client on the partnership approach and communicate the benefits of this approach in managing the change process.

7. What level of respect does the client have for the individual IS consultant heading up the project and for other key IS personnel involved in the project? How comfortable does he or she feel that these people will be successful?

What you can do: Develop strategies to assure the client that he or she is in capable hands. Involve consultants who have a positive track record with the client or, if this is impossible, use them as quiet influencers to bolster client confidence.

8. How disruptive is the change perceived to be to ongoing work? The degree of resistance is often directly proportional to the amount of disruption the users of the system think will be caused by the new system. And if you do not pay attention to this issue through a constant flow of information to these users, their perception of the coming disruption will be defined by the grapevine.

What you can do: Work with the managers of the affected users so that they have realistic expectations of the effects on current work, and develop plans to manage the transition.

9. Is the change proceeding at the right pace? Change that is too fast can generate resistance as resentment builds up over the unavoidable increase in workload to absorb the change. Change that is too slow is equally dangerous; as momentum drops, confidence in the project's success can wane, and concern about failure can lead to resistance.

What you can do: Work with management when defining project schedules to account for concerns about pace. Test as the project proceeds to ensure that pace is appropriate in all affected areas.

10. Does the learning curve seem manageable in view of other tasks? What is the client's comfort level that his or her organization can absorb the new system without losing control of other tasks? You must be sensitive to the fact that any one project, however important, is only one item on the client's plate.

What you can do: Ask clients what their workload looks like for the duration of the project. Work with them to accommodate the project to this reality, including business cycles, other major change commitments, staff absences, and other factors affecting the organization's ability to absorb change.

11. What fear of failure exists? How confident is the client in the success of the project? Fear of failure can lead to resistance even when the client is in favor of the change itself.

What you can do: Work from the beginning of the project to build client confidence. Be frank and honest about the risks so the client does not feel you are concealing them. Work together to develop strategies for managing the risks. Continue to test for anxiety about failure as the project proceeds.

12. Have client concerns for information availability, integrity, and security been addressed? Whenever an existing system is replaced or significantly modified, clients have concerns that accessibility or reliability of their data will be affected. In many cases the client trusts the information he or she gets from the existing system; years of experience have enabled the client organization to understand the system, learn to live with its quirks, and know how to work with the data it provides. Even when the new system promises significant improvements in timeliness and flexibility, the client is trading a comfortable known for an unknown.

What you can do: Build these issues into the project plan by including demonstrations of the system's integrity, security and availability features—and don't wait until acceptance testing. Plan for parallel testing or parallel operation to allow the client to test the new products against the old familiar ones.

13. Is good two-way communication with the client maintained throughout the project? Staying in touch regularly is the best preventive for resistance. Concerns can surface and be addressed as they arise and prevented from developing into major issues.

What you can do: Build communication into the partnership contract (see Chapter 6). Be honest about project problems and risks to encourage the client to be frank about concerns. Use this checklist to test for potential resistance at project startup, and then recheck at regular intervals throughout the project.

A STRATEGY FOR MANAGING RESISTANCE

No matter how well you manage the change process, clients will sometimes resist. What you need in these cases is a strategy for dealing with the resistance through the client/consultant relationship. Your goal in working with resistance is to *turn hidden agendas into solvable problems*. If you keep this problem-solving orientation, you are less likely to take the resistance personally or to get off the track. Resistance is good, valuable information: it tells you about an aspect of the client's problem that you did not understand. Getting the resistance out on the table, where it can be worked on in partnership, is the mark of a good IS consultant.

Here is a simple five-step strategy for working with your client to get resistance out on the table.[1]

Step 1. Develop a Client Profile

Seeing the situation as the client sees it enables you to predict client concerns and sources of resistance. Profiling Frank, the client in the example at the beginning of this chapter, shows how this can work. Frank had been managing a mail room operation for 10 years and was extremely comfortable with all aspects of the process. Replacing internal mail distribution with a completely new automated process threatened his sense of control over a large part of his job. Furthermore, the process currently worked well, at least from his perspective; the introduction of a radically different and technically complex method of distributing mail opened up the door to major and unforeseeable risks of failure and of problems he could not remedy. And these concerns, coupled with the pressure of the management edict, fed a fear that the project was at bottom a strategy to move him out the door by giving him

---

[1]Our approach to managing resistance has been influenced by Peter Block's treatment of the subject in *Flawless Consulting* (see Appendix).

a responsibility he couldn't handle. Seeing the issues from the client's perspective is the first step in dealing effectively with resistance when it comes up.

Step 2. Identify Symptoms of Client Resistance

Resistance is by definition indirect, but the symptoms are usually clear. In identifying symptoms, focus on specific behaviors that are blocking or slowing down the process of change. The resistance can be expressed verbally:

- Defiance: "There's no way I'll use this report."
- Resentment: "Oh, great. Just what we need. Another terrific idea from management."
- Power play: "I've been in this business 17 years and let me tell you . . .".
- Blaming: "If Donna would just follow through . . .".
- Giving in: "Well, if you say so."
- Forming alliances: "We got together after work and decided . . .".
- Withdrawing: "Look, I'd love to help out on this, but I'm just too busy."

Nonverbal behavior can also be a symptom:

- Sulky, withdrawn, unusually quiet.
- Defensive, self-protective.
- Touchy, contrary.
- Avoiding eye contact.
- Anxious.
- Complaining.
- Sarcastic, ridiculing, smirking.

Client action (or inaction) can also indicate resistance. Putting off meetings on the project, or not following through on project-related tasks, may be a signal that all is not well and that the client is simply avoiding the source of his or her discomfort. A drop in the energy level the client brings to the project may also be a signal. Even agreement can be a form of resistance—agreement that comes too quickly, too easily on a difficult issue; agreement that comes with no sense of commitment; agreement in words that is not reflected in action.

Recognizing resistance often means reading between the lines. "Gut feeling" is your best friend here. Trust your intuition and depend on it for constant monitoring of client interactions. It is also important to separate areas of true disagreement from patterns of client reluctance that don't seem logical. The client has the right to disagree. Open disagreement requires clarification and negotiation, but it is not resistance.

Step 3. Bring the Resistive Behavior to the Client's Attention in Nonblaming, Nonemotional Terms

The most basic way to get the resistance out on the table is to describe it to the client honestly and forthrightly. But this must not be done in blaming language that creates defensiveness. Explain that your role in the process is to help get things unstuck.

In Frank's case, Sue could respond to his getting off the track using these words:

> "It seems that each time we begin defining your current operations, you return to talking about the management mandate for the project."

Or, to deal with his implicit suggestion that the project could not succeed:

> "It seems that you have serious doubts that we can make this project work."

Both statements are nonjudgmental, straightforward descriptions of the communication. They do not argue that the client is wrong or out of line. They are not defensive. Rather, they are invitations to address the issues underlying the resistance more directly.

Step 4. Allow the Client to Respond

Create the right atmosphere for the client to share his or her concerns. Follow your invitation with a real chance for the client to bring the issue out on the table. Communicate through a pause and attentiveness a real willingness to hear the concerns. You are also sending your client a message that you will not let indirect communication like this continue—you will do your part to keep the communication honest and open.

The client may, in fact, not be fully aware of the resistance and its causes and may need some time to think about how to respond. The patience you show in waiting is a mark of respect for the client. In many cases it will pay off royally, as the client responds with valuable information on the cause of the resistance. Occasionally your question will clarify a concern that the client had not fully understood, and the resulting discussion will be a relief for both. Or the client may begin with words such as, "I didn't want to bring it up, but . . ." and go on to describe a problem that has led him or her to feel uneasy about the project.

Step 5. Work in Partnership to Clarify the Client's Concerns and Negotiate Mutually Agreeable Solutions

Once you are unstuck, and the problem behind the resistance is out on the table, it can be addressed. This means that the problem must be taken seriously, a process that may involve redefining the contract, reworking schedules, reassigning resources, and other major changes in the project plan. But at least the project process is unstuck. A quick and sure attack on the problems surfaced, using some of the suggestions in the checklist above, is the best cure for resistance. If you are successful, trust and motivation will be boosted and the client will be more likely to share similar concerns in the future.

CHAPTER 14

PUTTING THE TOOLS TO WORK: DEALING WITH DIFFICULT CLIENT SITUATIONS

Building partnership with a cooperative, motivated, technology-literate client is one thing; doing it under pressure, with an irate, mistrustful, or sabotaging client is another. Yet getting things done in less than ideal circumstances is business as usual for most IS consultants, and the tools and techniques we have presented are not much help if they can't get you through the tough times. This chapter presents three scenarios where IS consulting skills are put to the test. For each scenario we've included some specific guidelines for consulting behavior that can turn the problems around.

OPEN SEASON ON IS

The Situation

An MRP II (integrated manufacturing system) project. Basic design decisions have been made, including purchase of an MRP II package from a major vendor. The project team is now working to tailor several modules of this package, one of which is focused on materials management. The consultant is holding the first design meeting with representatives of the materials department in their conference room.

The Players

Fred: A materials manager, not the primary client, but a key information source for this module.

Tom: Materials staff member.
Mary: The IS consultant, lead systems analyst on this module.
Joe: A programmer/analyst who works for Mary.

The Action

MARY:
> As you all know, we are here today to begin collecting your input on module 3 of the MRP II system. Before we get started, let's review the agenda and objectives I forwarded to you.

FRED:
> [*Sitting forward in his chair, arms crossed and elbows resting on the conference table.*] Is this going to take long?

MARY:
> No longer than we discussed on the phone on Wednesday—about an hour. Do you have a conflict?

FRED:
> I have a problem with wasting time with you data systems people when you can't even deliver a decent product.

MARY:
> What product are you concerned about?

FRED:
> You guys can't even handle the systems you have, much less this MRP stuff!

What You Can Do

Yes, it's open season on IS. Mary is in a tough position. She is hearing harsh and grossly generalized criticism of IS. If she gets emotionally hooked, her first reaction is likely to be defensive. She is also likely to get frustrated quickly, because it looks like she may be in for a time-wasting battle. She is there to get down to the details about the materials module. She has done her homework and is prepared to make good use of the client's time. But the client just wants to complain about some vague problems with IS!

Rule number one for Mary at this point is not to get hooked emotionally. We are not suggesting that she ignore her emotional reaction—it provides valuable data about what is going on. We simply don't want her to get pulled into an emotion-laden exchange that will not be productive and will likely heighten the conflict. Let's see if some consulting tools can help her.

Think about the context of the meeting. Though the project is well underway, this is Mary's first meeting with this client and the first meeting on this system module. So Mary is really in an *initial contact* situation here. One of the rules of initial contact (Chapter 5) can help her avoid getting hooked: **Profile the client.**

It is almost impossible to get caught up in your own emotional reaction if you are focusing your attention on the client. And the client is givng Mary quite a bit of information in these first three sentences. We can use this information to profile him:

- He doesn't see the value of the meeting.
- His body language indicates real pressure and anger.
- He doesn't have confidence in IS (or in Mary as IS's representative and a personal unknown).
- He seems to have major doubts about the success of the MRP II project.

This is simply a paraphrase of what Fred said, with a bit of basic observation thrown in. If Mary can focus on the client and get this far with an on-the-fly client profile, she will avoid getting hooked emotionally.

The next consulting tool that can help Mary is the shared meeting agenda from Chapter 7. She knows what her meeting agenda is, and her client had agreed to it on the phone. But what is his meeting agenda right now? It obviously has some items on it that she knows nothing about. And his frustration and anger are strong enough to prevent any progress on her agenda items until his are addressed. What Mary wants to avoid, above all, is an unproductive meeting, especially one that turns into a debate about the merits or demerits of IS. But until she finds out what is on Fred's agenda this morning, she can go nowhere.

Mary needs to get beyond the negative generalizations about IS. She cannot take any productive action based on them. She also needs to avoid fanning the flames so that she can get Fred to make his agenda more specific. An open-ended question can accomplish both goals:

MARY:

It seems that something related to IS has you pretty frustrated. Is there a particular problem on your mind?

FRED:

> My materials reports on the SNAZZ project have been late three weeks in a row, and my people have been working overtime just to keep things from blowing up! You guys just can't do anything right. I'm pretty fed up, and now you want more of my people's time for this pie-in-the-sky project.

Now Mary is getting somewhere. The negative generalizations continue, but she's got one specific agenda item. She needs to verify it and keep the focus on specifics.

MARY:

> You mentioned the late SNAZZ reports. Are there any other items that are causing you problems?

FRED:

> Yeah. I've had a terminal out of commission in my area for two weeks now. I have four of my materials people doubling up on one tube and they're at each others' throats. Tom here can't even get on the tube to check the status of the electronics for the WIMS contract, and management is breathing down my neck to get that stuff to the factory no matter what. You guys are just a big headache for me.

MARY:

> Other than the late reports and the down terminal, are there any other items you can think of?

FRED:

> [*Pause*]: No, that's it right now . . . , but who knows what it will be next week.

Now, we have a clear client agenda. Fred's frustration with his late reports and malfunctioning terminal makes him low on trust and motivation to deal with Mary's agenda. Mary and the MRP project team have nothing to do with these problems—they are operations and technical support issues. Mary's group doesn't even work in the same building as the groups that handle those issues. But Mary knows that she will only increase Fred's frustration by telling him that's not her job, or by agreeing that those dolts in operations can't do anything right. In order to get some action on her agenda items, she will need to put something concrete on the table to deal with Fred's. And she senses that promises and discussion are not going to do the job. She needs to show Fred some action that will begin to build some credibility for her and her project team. Luckily, she has Joe in the meeting and can get some action going without disrupting the meeting.

MARY:

> Joe, I'd like you to take whatever time you need right now to see what we can do to address these two issues for Fred. [*Joe gets up and leaves.*] We'll add to the agenda some action reports from Joe on those two issues, because we certainly can't have you contributing to this project the way we want you to if you have those kinds of operational problems.

By carefully choosing her language, Mary has removed the complaints from the context of negative generalizations about IS and put them in the context of the partnership relationship she wants to have with Fred. And by taking action on Fred's operational problems, she has dissipated some of Fred's resistive energy, built some credibility, and shown Fred that she wants to focus on solvable problems. She has also displayed a professional and client-focused image of the IS group.

But she is still not done with agenda issues. There is an implicit item on Fred's agenda. It needs to be put on the table. Here the guidelines on dealing with resistance in Chapter 13 come into play.

MARY:

> And I'd like to suggest we add another item to the agenda today, Fred. Your comments about MRP II suggest that you have some real concerns about the viability of this project. If that's true, I'd like to hear those before we get into the other items on the agenda.

Mary has quickly redefined the agenda, by hearing, clarifying, and adding the client's agenda items and has set the stage to begin the body of the meeting by directly addressing Fred's implicit concerns about the project.

FRED:

> [*Pauses, sits back in his chair, sighs. His tone changes abruptly, now sounds tired, frustrated.*] Look, I know management is behind this project and that it's going to happen. But I have to tell you, my people are hearing all this stuff through the rumor mill that has them panicked about this MRP thing. They don't see how they're going to get through this and still do their jobs. I'm fighting every day to just keep them going, and they spend half their time sweating about this new system that's going to make them crazy or put them out of work. And I don't know enough about it to tell them what's going to happen.

MARY:

> So you and your group are both feeling a lot of anxiety about the new system, and that anxiety is fueled by the newness of the MRP concept and uncertainty about how it's going to affect your jobs.

FRED:

Yeah, that's a big part of it. And I have to tell you, when I can't even get reports on time or get a terminal fixed, I've got big concerns about how you guys are going to manage a project this huge. We're swimming hard just to keep above water now. If this thing comes in and fails, I just don't know how we're going to survive.

MARY:

MRP II is a big, complex system. Our project leader, Jim Feltzer, has installed MRP II successfully at four other electronics firms, and he echoes your concerns exactly. Making sure that the implementation is manageable by the front-line staff is one of the main criteria for success. In fact, one of the things we'll be doing over the next several meetings is getting a clear picture of your constraints and your schedule, so we can build an implementation plan that is manageable.

Based on what I'm hearing, Fred, I'd like to suggest another item for the agenda. We need to discuss some means of briefing you, and then your staff, on MRP II and how it will impact your group. I'd like to address your concerns directly, and I see no reason why we can't do that within a week or two.

FRED:

You really think this project is going to fly?

MARY:

The system we're installing is working right now at King Manufacturing, which has a fairly similar environment. There are some tough problems facing us, but we've got a solid team of manufacturing people and IS people working to tailor it to our environment. The commitment is there from management, as you said—and they are not pushing for an unrealistic schedule. They want this done right.

Mary gave Fred a chance to air his concerns, verified them, and then showed how they will be addressed during their work together. She did not try to minimize their importance. This gives Fred enough confidence to focus on the agenda of the current meeting. [*Fred sits back in his chair as Joe returns.*]

MARY:

Let's stop and see what Joe has found out.

JOE:

Fred, Tom, your new terminal arrived DOA from the vendor last week, and the vendor promised a replacement in a few days, but it hasn't been delivered yet. In the meantime, we've identified a terminal that can be used as a loaner, and I have our tech support people working to transfer it right now. Tom, you can contact Gina at 3448 if you have any questions on that.

On the reports, I spoke with our operations manager, Klaus, and with Rich Thompson in scheduling. They're tied up today, but they have scheduled a meeting with your SNAZZ coordinator, Marge, for tomorrow morning to resolve that lateness problem. I have asked Klaus to update you tomorrow, Fred. And I'll touch base with you tomorrow to make sure we're on top of these two problems.

With a little extra effort and a little luck, Joe managed to get some action moving on Fred's problems. Even if he hadn't been able to get action that quickly, the very act of leaving the meeting sent the right message to Fred. Mary has sent two other important messages in this short exchange: she wants to deal with tough issues directly, and she is willing to adjust to her client's needs. Now Mary has the resistance out on the table, has built some credibility for making things happen, and has Fred ready to work on the problem in partnership.

THE NOT-SO-QUIET INFLUENCER

The Situation

Recommendations/decision making stages of an end-user computing project. The IS consultant has investigated options and made some recommendations. Things have gone smoothly up to this point. The next step is a meeting with the client to review the options and discuss next steps.

The Players

Patrick: The IS consultant, an information center analyst. Works on corporate staff.

Edna: The client, a first-line supervisor in a division.

Randy: A systems analyst in Edna's division.

The Action

Patrick arrives at Edna's office, where they have agreed to meet to discuss Patrick's recommendations.

PATRICK:
> Hello, Edna, are you ready for our 9:00 meeting?

EDNA:
> Yes, Patrick. [*Gathers up her notes and moves toward the door.*] We're going to meet in Randy's office today.

PATRICK:
> [*Confused*]: Who is Randy?

EDNA:
> He's on the IS staff here. He was helpful in reviewing your recommendations, and I thought it would be good to involve him in the meeting.

Patrick, puzzled, is silent as they walk to Randy's office. When he gets to the office, he introduces himself.

PATRICK:
> Hello, Randy. Edna tells me you are here to discuss the system we're going to implement in her area.

RANDY:
> You won't implement it if I can help it.

Patrick, thrown off guard by Randy's remark, tries to ignore it and turns to Edna.

PATRICK:
> Edna, last time we met we discussed your needs and had agreed on the basics of a solution, isn't that correct?

RANDY:
> [*Cutting her off*]: She didn't agree to anything. Where did you get this recommendation anyway?

What You Can Do

Patrick has run into a not-so-quiet influencer, and it hurts. The action so far is rich with information about the situation Patrick is stuck in. If we profile the players, we see that Edna:

- Has conferred with Randy and invited him to the meeting without informing Patrick.

- Has moved or agreed to move the meeting location to Randy's office.
- Has so far played a rather passive role in the meeting.

Patrick can only infer the meaning of this behavior until he gets more data, but it appears that Edna either does not have confidence in Patrick's recommendations, or does not have confidence in her own ability to evaluate them. Her passive role so far suggests the latter. Whatever the source of her concern, she is obviously uncomfortable raising the issues with Patrick—a classic case of client resistance.

In our brief exposure to Randy, we see that he:

- Seems to have major concerns about the solution option Patrick has developed.
- Came out shooting, taking a very aggressive and confrontational approach to Patrick.
- Questions Patrick's credibility.

Randy is harder to read, since Patrick has no history with him to draw on. Why is he coming on so strong? Is it one-upsmanship to establish his own credibility? There is no way to know until we can develop a better profile.

Two environmental factors play a role in this scenario: a distrust of corporate staff in the divisions, and a lack of communication and work relationship between traditional IS groups and the end-user computing support staff in the information center.

Patrick also needs to realize that he was thrown off balance when he came to Edna's office and again when he felt the sting of Randy's first remark. At the point where we left him, he has lost control of the meeting, and his credibility is sinking.

To regain his balance, Patrick needs to keep several consulting issues in mind:

1. Patrick thought he was at the decision-making stage of the consulting cycle. Edna's resistance and Randy's appearance are strong indicators that he needs to loop back, probably to the contracting stage. The original contract was made with Edna; that contract has been changed by Edna through the introduction of Randy. Unless Patrick can eliminate Randy from the picture (which seems unlikely), the contract must be renegotiated, with Randy included.

2. Patrick needs to get Edna's resistance out on the table. He will have difficulty doing that with Randy taking such an aggressive stance.

3. Patrick needs to regain facilitative control of the meeting before he can accomplish anything productive.

How to deal with Randy's attacks on Patrick's credibility is perhaps the toughest judgment call. It is on the surface a personal attack on Patrick. What can he do?

Patrick decides that he will confront Randy about his remark but not in front of the client. He decides to address the credibility issues Randy is raising through action rather than words. He stands up and goes to the white board in Randy's office and picks up a marker. He wants to put the focus back on the problem and manage Randy long enough to describe Edna's resistance in neutral terms:

PATRICK:

Randy, it seems that you have some serious concerns about the recommendation for Edna's system. I want to hear what those are in just a minute. Edna, it seems to me that you're not comfortable with making a decision on this system yet.

EDNA:

Well, I thought it would be a good idea to get our IS group's opinion, and Randy seemed to have some problems with it.

With this preliminary verification of the problem, Patrick can go about making explicit the redefinition of the contract and get Edna's side of the redefinition—her needs—on the table.

PATRICK:

O.K. I came to this meeting prepared to move forward given your comfort with the recommendation, Edna, but I'm hearing from you that we haven't reached that point. And I'm also hearing that you value Randy's perspective on the project and would like him to be included in the evaluation of options. Is that accurate?

EDNA:

Yes.

RANDY:

Now, I don't have time to be part of your project team. I just have some real problems with this PC system you guys have put together.

PATRICK:

And I want to hear what those are. I don't think it's necessary for you to be a full-fledged project team member on this, Randy, but if we are going to examine options together, I need a commitment from you to spend some time with me on this. Here's how I propose we proceed: I suggest we use the rest of this meeting to (1) capture a list of Randy's concerns about the project and (2) walk through a quick recap of Edna's needs so that we are working from a mutual understanding of the problem. Then, Edna, I think Randy and I should meet to assess the technical options and develop a list of pros and cons for those options. Then the three of us will meet again to discuss those options, and we will spend as much time as you need to feel comfortable making a decision. Edna, how do you feel about that plan?

EDNA:

That sounds O.K., if Randy can do it.

PATRICK:

Randy, I'm asking you to commit to two more meetings after this one.

RANDY:

[*Sighs*]: All right.

Patrick has accomplished quite a bit in this five minutes. By standing up and taking a marker at the white board, he reestablished facilitative control—not to cut Randy off, but to get things back on track. And the very act of standing up and controlling the white board helped him regain his mental balance and focus on the problem. Again, not getting hooked emotionally is key to his ability to maintain a problemsolving focus. It enables him to manage Randy by showing him he wants to hear, and indeed list, his concerns. The worst approach would have been to begin to defend his recommendation and argue about his concerns point by point. The resulting debate would do nothing but sour the client further.

Once Patrick has clarified the resistance, he can proceed to the job of recontracting. Notice how Patrick makes this recontracting explicit—using the stages of the consulting cycle to bring home the implications of the change Edna has made. A key part of the contract is the roles the participants will play, and Patrick makes it clear that from his point of view, the new contract won't work with Randy in the role of not-so-quiet influencer, attacking the project from the sidelines. He needs to be directly involved in the process.

Patrick's suggested plan sets the discussion of technical options in a separate meeting with Randy giving Patrick and Randy a chance to settle their differences and develop a presentation that will help Edna feel more comfortable with the technical side of the decision. It also gives Patrick a chance to surface and address the issues underlying his aggressive approach.

CAUGHT BETWEEN A BOSS AND A HARD PLACE

The Situation

A programmer/analyst is working on a series of sales reports for the sales manager, who has reviewed and approved a set of specifications for the reports and agreed to the timetable proposed by the programmer/analyst.

The Players

Mario: A programmer/analyst.
Gus: A street-smart, get-things-done sales manager.
Linda: Manager of systems development, sales and marketing systems, Mario's supervisor.

The Action

Mario has finished coding the new reports and has begun testing using sample sales data. On his desk yesterday morning, Mario found a handwritten note from Gus attached to a marked-up copy of the report specifications. The note described some changes he wanted to make to the reports. Mario analyzed the proposed changes and set up a meeting.

GUS:
   I'm sorry about these last-minute changes, Mario, but there's nothing I can do. We need this additional information, and I just couldn't foresee that when we agreed on the specs.
MARIO:
   I've reviewed the changes, Gus, and I don't see any problems implementing them, but you realize that we won't be able to make the original due date for the reports. These are substantial changes that will take some time. I've prepared a revised timetable, and I think we can have them all completed by adding a month to the original schedule.
GUS:
   Well, yeah. Let me think about that; I'll get back to you.

Mario sensed that Gus was not happy with this revised date, but didn't want to back down from what he knew was as tight a schedule as he could handle to finish the changes. The meeting ended.

Later the same day, Gus stopped by to see Linda.

GUS:

You know, Linda, I'm really pleased with the work you people are doing on this project. These new reports are really going to help us. Now, I need to add a few things to the report formats. These changes are absolutely critical. I'm getting pressure from the v.p. of sales. He wants these changes and he wants them quick; we can't afford to let the original deadline slip. I hope you can make that deadline, or I will have some serious problems.

LINDA:

I'm sure that won't be a problem. Mario is one of our best programmers. He'll get the job done.

Later that day, Linda checked with Mario to make sure the original timetable would be met.

MARIO:

Linda, there's no way I can meet that timetable. Besides, I met with Gus and gave him a revised timetable. He said he'd get back to me.

LINDA:

It's too late for that now. We've got the v.p. of sales pushing for this. We have to make the deadline.

What You Can Do

One of the most common and aggravating problems in systems development is those last-minute, just-a-few-little changes to a system specification. Add to that a boss who is making promises to a client without your involvement and a client who is going over your head to get what he wants, and you have a real consulting challenge.

Mario was furious. His first inclination was to complain to Linda about doing things behind his back. Instead, he went back to his desk to clear his head. "How could they do this to me?" was his first thought. It seemed ridiculously unfair.

Let's look at Mario's situation to see what consulting tools can help him. He is actually on the right track with his question. How could they do this to him? He needs to profile his client and his boss to understand things from their perspective—to use empathy. Let's start with the client. Why would Gus go over his head like that? Mario came up with an idea.

1. Gus is a political schemer and will do anything to get his way just for the fun of it.

This one made Mario feel good. But it didn't give him any way out of his problem. So he thought some more.

2. Gus had promised the reports to his v.p. by the original date, doesn't feel he can deliver them without the changes, and doesn't feel comfortable going to the v.p. to get an extension. He couldn't think of any other way to deal with the problem but to put pressure on Linda.
3. Gus doesn't believe me when I tell him that I need an extra month to make the changes.

These two options started him thinking about ways to attack the problem. The first thing that came to mind was his own experience a week earlier. He had taken his car to a new auto mechanic for repair. Mario knew basic car maintenance, but he didn't know the ins and outs of major repairs. When the mechanic told Mario he needed a new clutch that would cost $500, Mario felt a twinge in the pit of his stomach. He felt like he was at the mercy of the mechanic because he didn't know enough about automotive technology to judge the mechanic's diagnosis. Gus was a new client for Mario; maybe he felt the same way about Mario's estimates. Maybe he felt going to Linda was the only way to ensure he was getting the best service he could.

Now for Linda. Why had she reacted the way she had? He worked on some ideas:

1. Linda is an incompetent and spineless manager who won't stand up for her employees.

But he knew this wasn't true. Linda had made a management error in making a contract without all parties present. But there was no way to change that now. And he didn't think he could discuss the issue with Linda until he found a solution to the problem with Gus. He tried putting himself in her shoes, sitting behind her desk when Gus came in. This generated some more ideas:

2. Gus had caught her off guard and had probably made the changes sound minor, because in his mind they were.
3. Gus was an influential client and she wanted to make sure that he and the v.p. were satisfied.
4. Linda wasn't really aware of the details of what he was working on.

These ideas got him thinking again of ways to attack the problem.

The consulting cycle provides a framework for focusing on this problem. When Gus asked for changes to the reports, he was asking for a new contract with Mario. Mario responded by laying out his requirements for the new contract—a deadline extension. But he didn't test for his client's understanding or comfort of that requirement. His sense of Gus's uneasiness, Gus's unexplained need to think over the new deadline, and his vagueness about when he would get back to Mario were red flags that they had no mutual agreement yet.

Then Gus went to Linda, and Linda reassured him that the changes would be made on the original schedule. Linda made a new contract with Gus, but a different one than Mario had asked for. Mario thought about going back to Gus to try to iron things out, but he now had a direct order from his boss to abide by the original deadline. Because Linda made the contract with Gus, Mario has to include her in his efforts to get the contract changed. Whatever he does, he needs to get her to buy in first.

How can he do that? By addressing her concerns and needs. Going back to his quick profile of her, Mario saw that she was most interested in satisfying Gus's needs. He also saw that she was not really aware of the details of his project. He put together a quick strategy and went back to Linda's office the next morning.

MARIO:

Linda, I have some real concerns about the project for Gus, and I need your help in working through my options. I know that Gus is a key client, and that his boss is pushing him for these reports. That's why I'm concerned. I know we're committed to getting these changes done by the original deadline, and I spent last night going over my plan to see how I could make it happen. I'm coming up blank, but I want to walk through the thought process with you to make sure I'm not missing something. It should take about 20 minutes.

LINDA:

> [*Looking very concerned*]: That's not what I wanted to hear, Mario, but let me see what you've got.

Mario walked Linda through his plan, making sure she understood and agreed with all his assumptions. When he was done she saw the difficulty he was in.

LINDA:

> You're right, Mario—this does look impossible. I never should have committed to those changes without checking with you.

Mario has succeeded in getting Linda to work in partnership with him on the project. With that partnership established, they can attack the problem creatively.

MARIO:

> When this is over, I think we can work out a way for me to keep you more informed about my work which may help prevent that kind of thing. But the important thing right now is to satisfy the client. I'd like to discuss our options for making the best of this difficult situation with Gus. I think we agree that if we proceed as is we will miss the deadline and face a real blow-up by the sales v.p. and Gus and take the blame for being unresponsive again.

LINDA:

> What if I assign another programmer to the job to help you?

MARIO:

> It would help on 2 of the 12 reports. In fact, we could realistically get 4 of the 12 done that way by the deadline. The rest are really going to require more time, and bringing someone else up on them would take just as long.

LINDA:

> Well, at least we can offer the client four of the changed reports by the deadline. What other options do we have?

MARIO:

> We can offer to implement all the other reports by the deadline without the changes, if that is of any value to them, and then implement the changes over the next month.

LINDA:

> Are they interested in that?

MARIO:

> That's one of the things we don't know—if their urgent need is for all the reports or a few.

LINDA:
So we really don't know what the urgency is. Is it possible that the v.p. has some specific needs for information coming out of these reports?
MARIO:
It's possible.
LINDA:
Well, if we find out that there is, we can offer Gus some support from the information center to get that information on a one-time basis.
MARIO:
That's a great idea. The calculations and procedures involved in the reports are not that complex. It's just that it takes time to build them in to the existing system on a production basis. The IC could use a file extract and one of their analysis tools to get them whatever specific data they need.
LINDA:
Well, I feel better. We have several options to offer.
MARIO:
I think we have another issue to address, though, in terms of how we approach Gus with this. I am only inferring from how he handled this, but it seems he is in a really tight spot with the v.p. Since we agreed to meet the original deadline, I think we should offer to tell the v.p. ourselves that we can't meet it.
LINDA:
Or go to the v.p. with him to discuss our options if he thinks that will help.
MARIO:
So we have the outline of a strategy for approaching Gus. Let me summarize:

1. Call Gus to ask for a meeting—the two of us will go to his office.
2. Explain the problem. I think an abbreviated form of the analysis I walked you through might help Gus see that we are not just arbitrarily making schedules—that there are real constraints on us. We'll have to be very clear on those.
3. Outline what we *can* offer him:
   a. Four reports by the deadline.
   b. All 12 reports minus the recent changes by the deadline.
   c. IC help in getting specific information until the changes are made.
4. Let him react and give us his understanding of their needs in terms of priority among the 12 reports or needs for specific information.
5. Offer to meet with the v.p. alone or with him to brief him on the problem.

The plan they have worked out together takes into account the three legs of the successful contract. It accounts for the technical limitations that make the original deadline impossible and adds some additional technical options (the information center) to meet the client's need. It addresses the vagueness (in Mario's and Linda's understanding, at least) of the business problem by building in a chance for Gus to clarify what he and the v.p. need most and for what purpose. And it addresses the messy work relationship with the client in two ways. First, Mario and Linda are acknowledging that they had made an agreement and had to back out of it. But they are willing to mitigate the negative effects of that by placing some offers on the table, including added programming resources and information center assistance for the short term. In addition, they are sending a clear message by appearing at the meeting together with a joint plan that Gus's "divide and conquer" approach will not work.

LINDA:

> One other issue—since I'm the one who told him we'd meet the deadline, I should be the one to set up that meeting.

Mario has succeeded in getting Linda's agreement on the new contract. Her volunteering to set up the meeting shows the level of her commitment. Now, presenting a unified message to Gus, they can get his participation in building a new contract they can all live with. The meeting with Gus will not be an easy one, but the results will be better than simply missing the deadline. Gus will probably react negatively to not getting what he asked for, but Mario and Linda are sending a message about how they want to do business—in partnership.

PART 4

PROACTIVE PARTNERING: MARKETING IS SERVICES

CHAPTER 15

IS MARKETING: ALIGNING IS SERVICES WITH CLIENT NEEDS

As IS organizations move into the problem-solving partnership role, marketing becomes an integral part of the IS professional's responsibilities. Marketing in this context does not mean selling or pushing IS products and services; it means aligning IS products and services to c ient needs, and then building an awareness of those products and services among the client community.

FOUR REASONS TO MARKET

Marketing serves four purposes for the IS organization trying to build a problem-solving partnership environment:

Clarifying Roles. Building an awareness of the role of the IS function in helping the organization use technology to take advantage of business opportunities, and the role of clients in taking more responsibility for information systems efforts.

Building Relationships. Fostering ongoing two-way communication about business needs and solid problem-solving relationships with the client areas.

Communicating Benefits. Enhancing the organization's understanding of what IS technologies can do for the business.

Targeting Opportunities. Identifying high-payoff opportunities for application of IS technology.

Marketing based on these objectives is a dynamic, two-way communication process that helps IS maintain that crucial alignment between its offerings and client needs. It helps IS stay aware of what is going on in the business environment, and it helps ensure that clients have the information they need to work in partnership with IS.

FOUR MARKETING "DON'TS"

Some IS professionals are uncomfortable with the very idea of marketing—to them it smacks of Madison Avenue hype. And the wrong kind of marketing can in fact do more harm than good. Usually, negative effects from marketing are a result of violating one of these four "don'ts":

Don't market technologies—market business solutions. Marketing should only address technology specifics when clearly requested by the client. Marketing should address clear business results, and in the client's terms.

Don't market yourself personally. This applies to anyone handling the marketing effort. Market your staff, your organization, and the business payoff of your services. Marketing that is (or sounds) self-serving will not foster partnership.

Don't sweep past failures or shortfalls under the rug. Be prepared to address them openly and confidently. These shortfalls are probably being discussed when you are not in the room to address them. The marketing effort provides a forum where they can be opened to dialogue. It is hard to build partnership on a foundation of past disappointments, but it is even harder to build one on a foundation of mistrust and misunderstanding.

Don't push IS services on anyone. Partnership, not salesmanship, is the key. Even a soft sell can short-circuit the process of building joint understanding of problems.

The rapidly changing business environment, the earned negative reputation IS has in many organizations, and the critical need for better application of information technology make marketing an absolute necessity for IS groups today. The biggest excuse among IS managers and professionals for *not* marketing is, "We're already swamped." Yet this is precisely where marketing can help the most. Effective marketing can actually help in managing IS overload and ensure that IS resources are applied where they will do the most good. A strong marketing campaign enables IS to focus more resources on the activities that further its mission.

It is not just the responsibility of IS management to make sure IS marketing happens. Each member of the IS team, especially the IS consultants with front-line exposure to clients, must make marketing a full-time responsibility.

ESTABLISHING A MARKETING BASELINE

A marketing map can give you a baseline snapshot of how well your products and services are aligned with client needs. The marketing map can be developed for IS as a whole or for subgroups. It is most effective when done as a team effort with a selection of people from the IS staff representing broad exposure to the organization as well as experience in different areas of IS.

First, draw a grid. The vertical columns of the grid will represent your clients, the vertical departments or groups within the organization. The horizontal rows will represent your products/services. You will need to decide what level of detail to use in creating the map. The columns can represent whole client departments or subgroups within departments. (Use an organization chart to map these quickly.) The rows should represent the breakdown of products and services that fits your organization. They might represent:

- Broad categories of service (e.g., system development, end-user computing support, consulting).
- Major types of applications (e.g., production, decision support, competitive impact).
- Individual applications (e.g., financial modeling, statistical analysis, online budgeting, customer database).
- Technology resources (e.g., local area networks, mainframe computing, workgroup computing).

Spend some time arguing over the categories—you will probably find real value in wrestling with just what you are in business to do.

Once you have constructed your grid, fill it in by indicating where you have made a match—where your products/services have met a real client need and are currently being used. How you fill in the grid will depend on how you want to use the chart. Where you have a match you can simply put a checkmark, or, to provide more data, fill in the name of the client or client group, or use ranking criteria such as high/medium/low to indicate the impact or effectiveness of the match. The end product is a graphic representation of where your IS group has had an impact. And more than likely you will see some real gaps where you have not made any matches. There are basically two reasons for not making a match: you do not have a product/service that meets this client group's needs, or you have failed to make the group aware of available products/services that do meet their needs. It may take some investigation to find out which of these is the case. Both are marketing problems: the first can be solved by needs assessment and development of appropriate products or services, the second by a marketing effort to make the match happen.

TARGETING HIGH PAYOFF OPPORTUNITIES: THE ACTION FUNNEL

Most IS groups cannot hope to hit every client group; restrictions on resources and technologies make this unrealistic. If you have a responsibility to make sure your group is giving the organization-at-large the best payoff on information technology investment, you need to proactively target those areas where that payoff is likely to be highest. Another marketing tool, the action funnel (see Figure 15–1), provides a framework for this effort.

The action funnel takes you through the following steps to identify high-payoff opportunities:

1. *Where?* Identify the areas with the highest likelihood of using information technology to leverage business opportunities. You can start by ranking the client areas in the columns of your marketing map high/medium/low in importance. What areas are driving the company? What areas are receiving close attention from senior management? What areas are targeted for major change? In what areas are competitors producing key improvements? Of course, a solid knowledge of the organization is necessary to make this ranking work. If your group doesn't have the information to do it, find ways to get it. Strategic and operating plans, competitive analyses, and interviews with key managers are places to start. These high-payoff areas are where IS must be

FIGURE 15–1
The Action Funnel

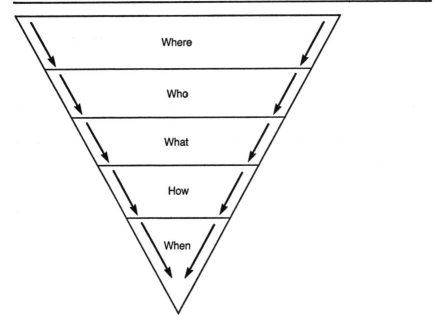

involved to give the organization the biggest return on its technology investment.

2. *Who?* Develop a partner map (see Chapter 10) for the area and identify the likely sponsors for information technology initiatives, the likely lobbying partners, the movers and shakers who will make successful problem-solving partners. How open are they to information technology efforts? Determine what access you already have to decision makers in the area, and what track record you can use to support your efforts. Who are the potential information partners to help you build on your preliminary analysis of the area's business situation?

3. *What?* Identify the key activities in the area and analyze your IS product/service mix for likely matches with the area's business needs.

4. *How?* Determine how you can best get entry into this area. How can you align your product/service mix to their needs? (The marketing approach described in Chapter 16 and some of the marketing methods outlined in Chapter 18 may be helpful here.) How will you proceed once you get them interested?

5. *When?* What timing is best for your entry? How do the area's business and budgetary cycles and your own resource availability dovetail to ensure the best results? What other resource-intensive efforts are they involved in that might make the timing bad? What other management initiatives are they working on that might provide momentum for an information technology effort?

Finally, be realistic about your marketing effort. Use the marketing map and the action funnel to identify three to five key areas to pursue with targeted marketing efforts and test the results by getting feedback from your clients. The key to ongoing success is ensuring that the marketing effort is really a two-way communication process designed to build and maintain partnership relationships.

CHAPTER 16

A SIMPLE MARKETING METHODOLOGY

One obstacle to meeting the four objectives of effective IS marketing —clarifying roles, building relationships, communicating benefits, and targeting opportunities—is a lack of experience and familiarity with marketing design. We have found that a simple three-stage methodology works well for all types of IS marketing efforts.

STEP 1: AUDIENCE PROFILE

Rule number one is know your audience. Marketing to a group of sales managers requires an entirely different approach than marketing to manufacturing supervisors. Develop an audience profile for the target group, including a list of key characteristics for the audience. This works whether the intended audience is a single manager, the supervisory staff of a department, or all clerical workers in the organization. It is best to generate this list in a brainstorming session involving anyone in IS who has experience with the client group. Figure 16-1 contains a sample audience profile for a marketing effort designed to promote a new standardized word processing/document distribution system.

STEP 2: POSITIVE AND RESISTIVE ISSUES

Based on the audience profile, develop:

1. A list of factors working in your favor in approaching this group, for example:

   a. Past IS successes with group members.
   b. Perceived need for technology support in the area.
   c. A top manager in the area who is a proponent of IS technology.
   d. High level of information technology knowledge among the staff.
2. A list of factors that may lead to resistance to your marketing effort, such as:
   a. Past conflicts with IS.
   b. Widely differing goals or agendas.
   c. Management who perceive little value in information systems.
   d. Little knowledge of the area's business in IS.

FIGURE 16–1
Audience Profile

Audience:

Mid-level engineering management in an electronics firm

Marketing effort:

Building support for a corporatewide word processing (WP) standardization using a product that runs on both personal computer (PCs) and mainframe computers.

Key characteristics:

- Project oriented: Tend to focus on needs of current customer/project.
- Schedule-driven: Concerned about any factors with potential to cause slippage in project deadlines.
- Budget-conscious: Worry over indirect versus direct labor costs as well as capital/expense budgets for group.
- Matrix Organization: Often "take orders" from project managers with widely differing priorities.
- Wide difference in age, background, experience with information technologies: Range from well-informed leading edge supporters to less interested skeptics.
- Conflict with IS: Often perceive IS as throwing roadblocks in their way and not understanding their specialized needs.
- Specialized needs: Widely varying requirements mean that one standard product will probably not meet all needs.
- Decentralized: Matrix organization and project orientation lead to lack of centralized planning or direction and wide variety of technology solutions.

The positive issues represent resources for the marketing effort. The resistive issues represent bases that should be covered in the marketing approach. Identifying the resistive issues up front enables you to do your homework in addressing the audience's concerns. Figure 16–2 contains a list of positive and resistive issues for the audience profiled above.

FIGURE 16–2
Positive and Resistive Issues

Positive Issues

- Mainframe WP package will be accessible via any terminal attached to local network, including terminals used to access engineering minis.
- New standard enables direct link between WP on PCs and terminals and corporatewide electronic mail and document filing/distribution system.
- Corporatewide electronic mail system has been specified by a major customer as delivery method for all documentation on upcoming large contract.
- New standard allows conversion from six major WP products used in engineering. Existing users of other packages need not change.
- New standard has similar user interface to the most commonly used WP system in engineering.
- New standard will be site-licensed and can be freely copied and distributed. Cost absorbed by IS budget for software.
- Requests for special-purpose products outside of standard must be clearly justified but will be considered.

Resistive Issues

- Difficulty of standardizing when customers on projects often request or demand specific IS products/environments as part of contract.
- Investment in existing WP systems.
- Introducing new product will cause delays in current projects due to learning curve.
- Frustration of learning "yet another new standard" will especially alienate technology skeptics.
- New standard will be perceived as meeting IS needs rather than engineering needs.
- New standard is not supported on many minicomputers used by engineers.
- Personal preferences in WP vary widely and are strongly defended. Engineering currently uses at least 12 WP products.

FIGURE 16–3
Strategy

Logistics:

Type of marketing effort:	Meeting/Demonstration
Duration:	150 minutes
Time:	Tuesday 8:45–11:15 A.M.
Place:	Small Engineering Auditorium (close to most engineering offices)
Media:	Text slides/demonstration on engineering type terminal linked to corporate mainframe, with screen image projected using ceiling-mounted projection
Audience:	15 engineering managers

Content:

Time	Module	Presenter
8:45–9:00	Coffee and danish	
9:00–9:10	Introduction	D. Truksus, Manager, Engineering support, IS

Introduction by the IS person most familiar to audience, who has good credibility from past projects.

Time	Module	Presenter
9:10–9:30	Decision process	J. Terrell, Engineering Manager

Explanation of decision process to select standard product, by engineering manager who was on task force. Specific coverage of engineering concerns (resistive issues) with explanation of decision tradeoffs and key selection criteria, following the process they use in making a design decision for an engineering contract.

Time	Module	Presenter
9:30–9:50	Project requirements	S. LeBouw, Project Director Major Customer, Inc.

A discussion of the role of the standard product in this customer's project plan, with explanation of reasons for their selecting the product.

Time	Module	Presenter
9:50–10:20	Demonstration	W. Weinstein, Engineer

A brief overview of the system's functions by an engineer who is a pilot user. He has prepared engineering design specifications on the mainframe system and downloaded them to a clerical support person's PC for cleanup. Demonstration ends with transfer of the document to the major customer's system via telecommunications.

Time	Module	Presenter
10:20–10:30	Question and answer session	All speakers
10:30–10:35	Software distribution	D. Truksus

IS hands out free copies of the PC version of the software to the managers, along with information on training and support.

Time	Module	Presenter
10:35–11:00	Additional informal demonstration and question and answer session	

STEP 3: STRATEGY

Use the audience profile and positive/resistive issues as a guide in developing a strategy for the marketing effort. The strategy should cover both the content and logistics of the approach. Logistics includes the who, where, when, and how of the marketing effort.

Content is the what—the actual issues to be covered. Make sure that the content section addresses major resistive issues and makes good use of the positive issues. The logistics section draws on the audience profile to determine the most effective vehicle, setting, players, and media for the marketing effort. Figure 16–3 contains a sample strategy for the marketing effort described above.

Note how the plan draws on the audience profile and positive/resistive issues to maximize the impact of the effort and manage the resistance. The presentation features heavy involvement by engineering personnel to minimize the "us-versus-them" conflict with IS indicated in the audience profile. It also uses a decision-review process that the audience is familiar with to address the resistive issues. The plan also takes advantage of a key positive issue by bringing in a respected project leader from the major customer organization that has standardized on the product and requires engineering to use it in delivery of contract-related documentation to the customer.

CHAPTER 17

THE IS MISSION STATEMENT

The foundation for your marketing efforts should be an IS mission statement. The mission statement, typically a short, carefully crafted summary of an organization's purpose, has been used by companies to create a common vision of what the organization is about for its staff and customers. The IS mission statement can do the same for your IS staff and clients.

BENEFITS OF A MISSION STATEMENT

In addition to providing that common vision, the mission statement:

- Sets a clear direction. This is especially valuable during times of major change.
- Sets and communicates goals. What is your IS group trying to achieve in the organization? The mission statement helps both you and your clients see these goals more clearly.
- Sets and communicates boundaries. What is inside and outside your charter? What do you do, and what don't you do? This is especially important in managing IS overload.
- Manages expectations. What can clients expect from you? What should they not expect from you? What do you expect from them?
- Builds a foundation for standards and procedures. Why did you set particular standards for hardware and software? Why do you work with clients the way you do? What roles do you play? The mission statement provides a central philosophy that supports standards and procedures.

Read these three mission statements and think about what they say about the IS organizations they represent:

1. The mission of Information Services is to provide systems development, maintenance, and computer operations in support of the XYZ Corporation business functions.

2. The mission of the Information Systems Division is to serve as an "information utility" to Alpha Corporation, providing computing and data communications power to our customers with the highest reliability and the lowest cost.

3. Our mission in Corporate Information Technology is to make ABC Inc. a leader in the industry by teaming with ABC clients to take advantage of business opportunities through the innovative use of information technology.

In one sentence, each of these statements shapes a very different image of an IS organization, with implications for the group's direction, goals, boundaries, and standards and procedures. This image is the foundation for marketing efforts, and one of the many benefits of the process of putting together a mission statement is that it forces you to think long and hard about what that image is now and what it should be to serve the organization most effectively.

Boiling the mission down to a single sentence helps you to focus your goals and simplify your message into something that can be easily communicated and remembered. This single-sentence mission should be supported by detail that fleshes out the mission and describes how you will accomplish it.

AN EXAMPLE

Figure 17–1 is an example of a mission statement that stresses the idea of partnership with the client areas in solving business problems

DEVELOPING AN EFFECTIVE
MISSION STATEMENT

The worst thing you could do in preparing a mission statement is to copy this one or anyone else's. Your mission should be based on the realities of the organization you work in, the goals and expectations of

FIGURE 17–1
Sample Mission Statement

The IS mission is to work in partnership with clients to leverage the use of information technologies to meet business challenges and to foster client self-sufficiency in using those technologies.

Goals

- Maintain a computing environment that supports clients in achieving their business objectives.
- Work with clients to establish and maintain a technology strategy and an information architecture that will serve the organization's current needs while maintaining flexibility to adapt to a changing environment.
- Work with client organizations to build the knowledge and skills they need to take full advantage of current and future technologies in their jobs.
- Work with clients to use information technology as an instrument in changing the business for the better.
- Minimize ongoing dependence on IS for the use of technologies.

Activities

To achieve these goals we work in partnership with the client community in the following activities:

- Information Technology/Business Planning.
- Consulting.
- Education and Training.
- Support.
- Evaluation, Selection, Acquisition, Installation, and Testing of Information Technologies.
- Maintenance of a centralized computing facility and data communications network.
- Development, Enhancement, and Maintenance of Applications.

Operating Philosophy

- Our charter is to coordinate, guide, and support the use of information technology in organization, not to control it. We strive to pave the way, not get in the way.
- Our relationship with business users is that of internal consultant to client.
- We work in partnership with clients because experience shows that the transfer of skills and knowledge to the client's group is as important as the development of technical solutions.
- IS is responsible for long-term information technology strategy, but that strategy must grow out of and serve the business needs of the clients.

senior management, the focus of the IS group, and the needs of the clients. The process of creating the IS mission statement is as important as its content. Many IS organizations have created mission statements that simply faded into oblivion shortly after development. When we go into an organization and ask for their IS mission statement, and someone pulls a dusty volume off the shelf, they have usually violated one of the rules for developing a mission that has lasting impact:

1. A mission statement built through a group effort that involves as much of the staff as possible has more chance of success than one created "on high" and enforced downward.

2. A process that includes IS subgroups writing their own mission statements that support the mission of the group above them has more chance of success.

3. Getting key clients involved in the development process produces a mission statement with more credibility. (It's never a bad idea to know what your customers want from you!)

4. A mission statement that everyone will get behind usually results from a development process where people fight about what their mission is and even about the wording and punctuation of the statement. If you haven't had that fight, people probably won't support the final product.

5. Having that fight takes time. Six months is not an unusual development period for a new mission statement.

6. A mission statement that is created and put on the shelf will do little good. Instead, put it on the wall, in the newsletter, in people's offices, in your marketing campaigns, in your talks with clients. The first step is for you to get excited about your mission; the second step is to get your clients excited.

7. Mission statements don't age well. They need to be revisited and, if necessary, revised, every 6 to 12 months. Your organization, your business, your staff, your focus, your technologies, your direction —all these things change. Don't let your mission statement fall behind.

8. If IS managers don't live the mission and take it seriously in their dealings with staff and clients, staff and clients won't take it seriously either.

If you work in an IS organization that does not have a mission statement, getting one developed can be a valuable consulting assignment, with real opportunity to hone your influence skills and build consensus for change.

CHAPTER 18

SUCCESSFUL IS
MARKETING APPROACHES

No specific marketing tool can work wonders; the key to success is a marketing orientation that recognizes and takes advantage of marketing opportunities, employing the methods and tools most appropriate to the situation. Use the following list to generate ideas for your own environment.

WALK-IN CENTER

The rise of the information center and end-user computing prompted many organizations to create a walk-in center where clients and prospective clients could receive face-to-face support with computing problems. The role of the walk-in center in some organizations has been expanded to become the "front door" for IS, the first point of contact for any client with questions or problems about the application of information technology to the business. In this capacity the walk-in center can play an important marketing function.

To take advantage of this opportunity, it is important to make marketing part of the walk-in staff's charter and make sure staff are trained in effective marketing methods. This training should include the goals of marketing, methods for handling walk-in traffic (which may include everyone from the top to the bottom of the corporate hierarchy and across every department), and guidelines on treating users as clients. Everyone who comes in should be treated with professional respect and genuine concern. The administrative help in the center should not be left out of this training. There will be times when the secretary will be the only person there to greet someone. He or she should be part of the marketing team.

Location

If you have the opportunity to set up a walk-in center from scratch, consider the location as a retail manager would. We all know a particular restaurant or retail store that goes through incarnation after incarnation with an empty parking lot, as if doomed to failure. Often it is the physical location that keeps customers away.

Layout

Like location, layout is a factor that will probably not help you sell but can hinder your efforts. Of course, what can be done in terms of an attractive and functional layout depends on the size and shape of the space and the furnishings and other resources available. Many walk-in centers begin as training or support centers and are designed that way, with emphasis on seating for trainees and a screen for overheads or slides. What is often lacking in such centers is an area that encourages walk-in business and serves as a consulting area for working with clients on an individual basis. Such an area need not be elaborate—a small section clearly visible from the door, separated from the training area by dividers, with room for two people to spread out their work comfortably is all that is needed.

CAPABILITIES PRESENTATION

Part of the walk-in center staff's training should include the ability to present a 10-minute introduction to IS that stresses how IS can be used as a resource by the client in meeting business goals. This pitch can be customized for different clients, but much of it will remain stable, making this a good place to invest a bit of time and money in professional-quality presentation aids. One of the most convenient and flexible media for such a presentation is large-format graphics produced on a plotter and mounted on a thick backing so they can stand on an easel. Personal computer or other graphics systems can also be used, but make sure that the logistics for getting the presentation started take no more than a minute or two; otherwise you can lose the customer's interest. This presentation should include slides on the following topics:

- The IS mission.
- Where IS fits in the organization.
- The IS staff groups and their responsibilities.
- IS's services.
- How IS works with clients.
- Technologies supported.

As with all IS marketing efforts, the emphasis should be on services and solutions, not particular technologies or systems, though a slide listing standard supported systems should be included near the end of the presentation. You can add a brief, preprogrammed, hands-on demonstration using equipment in the walk-in center to illustrate technology capabilities if the client is interested. Once the presentation is developed, train everyone on the walk-in staff to deliver it and to arrange for appropriate follow-ups.

SCHEDULED PRESENTATIONS

You can take the capabilities presentation on the road to various client groups to build awareness. A good opportunity for such a presentation is a 15-minute slot in the group's monthly staff meeting. For these presentations, augment the canned, general material developed for the walk-in center with a section addressing issues important to the group. This presentation can be a good tool for initiating contact with groups identified as critical in the marketing map.

BROWN BAG SESSIONS

An effective method for building a general awareness of IS, developing a service image, and building better communication with customers is the informal brown bag session. This is a presentation scheduled for a location in the client's area at lunch time. After clearing the session with the management of the area, send invitations asking people to bring their lunch and hear a presentation on some aspect of information technology. (It is a good idea to ask those invited to register by phone so that you can have a clear idea of the size of the audience and not over-book the room.) Make the setting relaxed, and make no demands on the attendees. This is an ideal method not only for educating clients in technology, but for hearing their concerns and questions in an informal setting.

Let different members of your IS staff participate in the brown bag sessions to build visibility for the staff as a whole and develop presentation skills for the team in this relatively non-threatening atmosphere. However, make sure that presenters are well prepared, practice their session in front of an audience, and have a good general understanding of technology issues in order to answer the wide-ranging questions that often come up in brown bag sessions.

Be careful to avoid all IS jargon in such sessions; here especially it is important to learn to discuss technology in terms that the audience understands. Brown bag sessions are the perfect opportunity to cultivate the ability to communicate an understanding and enthusiasm for technology to the business audience.

CAPABILITIES BROCHURE

A fundamental marketing and public relations tool for any consulting organization is a brochure describing the group's services, areas of expertise, and staff qualifications. This type of brochure can be very effective for IS, especially in large organizations. No matter how many times you make presentations, talk about your services, and train clients, people in the organization will forget, ignore the information because it does not meet their needs at the time, or be replaced. The capabilities brochure provides an ongoing, convenient tool for distributing to new hires, potential clients, and other interested parties.

The brochure can be similar in content to the IS presentation described in the section on the IS as Consulting Firm. It should include:

- The IS mission.
- Where IS fits in the organization.
- IS's services and how they work with clients.
- Staff and qualifications.
- Technologies/products supported.
- Location of walk-in facilities.
- Where to go for more information, including telephone numbers.
- An offer to give a presentation to interested parties to go into more detail on IS services.

This brochure should be revised at least once per year.

CLIENT HANDBOOK

An expansion on the capabilities brochure, the client handbook goes into more detail on IS services and provides additional information on standards, procedures, and facilities of interest to clients. Many IS organizations provide this handbook with each terminal or personal computer installed. Typical content in such a handbook includes:

- Descriptions of major application systems.
- Descriptions of training and support services.
- Forms and procedures for ordering and justifying end-user equipment and software.
- Forms and procedures for requesting IS services.
- Data security and auditing procedures for applications systems.
- Documentation forms and standards for client-developed applications.
- Descriptions of standard hardware/software products.
- The latest issue(s) of the IS newsletter, with room for filing additional issues.

This handbook provides real value for new clients as well as serving as a marketing tool. The problem with such handbooks is keeping delivered copies up to date. One way to do this is to make them loose-leaf and issue annual or as-needed updates. It may be preferable to maintain a list of clients who have the handbook and reissue it once a year, to eliminate the problem of clients not updating their copies.

COMPUTING ENVIRONMENT GUIDE

This publication has some similarities to the client handbook, but is designed more to build awareness and inform clients (and potential clients) about the big picture regarding information technologies in the organization. One of IS's most difficult tasks is keeping clients informed about the organization's current information architecture and the plans for future developments. We continue to lament the lack of technology planning among client groups, yet we so seldom provide them with information to help them integrate technology into their business plans. A computing environment guide can help in this effort. This is a report, written in clear, nontechnical language, that outlines the organization's information infrastructure. It should be designed to give existing and new employees the lay of the land regarding today's technical environment and the technical direction the organization is charting for meeting future needs.

Most people have limited knowledge of the entire information architecture in a large organization. Some may know a piece of it in detail and have only a shadowy notion of what other elements are involved. Especially in very decentralized organizations, this can lead to missed opportunities for sharing information and resources. The computing environment guide can help build bridges between these decentralized groups.

Your guide will get more attention if it is professionally produced, with effective graphics. Update it once a year to keep pace with changing technologies. Figure 18–1 is a sample outline for a computing environment guide.

NEWSLETTERS

Many IS newsletters are actually operational bulletins designed to alert programmers and technical system users of software updates, scheduled system maintenance, and other items affecting service on existing applications. As such they have minimal marketing value. With more effort, the newsletter can be used as a marketing tool to:

- Create an awareness of IS's role in promoting business success by highlighting client successes and stressing hard-nosed business results.
- Link IS efforts with business plans.
- Place IS efforts in a competitive context by comparing current or future systems initiatives with competitors' achievements.
- Educate clients about emerging technologies and their potential role in the organization.
- Build support for ongoing project efforts by providing progress reports, addressing concerns or resistance, and creating an awareness of benefits.

Of course, a newsletter that performs these functions requires more work on the part of the IS staff. If IS has been successful at building partnerships and encouraging technological self-sufficiency among client organizations, the newsletter can be prepared with the support of a group of contributing editors in key areas of the organization.

FIGURE 18–1
Computing Environment Guide

1. Table of Contents: On the cover, to make it easy to find needed information.

2. Management Introduction: Over the signature of the highest ranking IS executive, places the "Computing Environment Guide" in the context of the organization's overall business goals and competitive position.

3. Systems and Data Resources: A guide to applications systems and databases, arranged so that nontechnical users can find out which system contains data they need, and who to contact to find out more.

4. The Information Architecture: A description of the computing and telecommunications network supporting the services described above.

5. Computing Environments and Tools: Operating environments and software tools such as fourth-generation languages and report writers, with examples of their use.

6. The IS Organization: Describes the makeup of IS with an organization chart and profiles each subgroup and their charter, responsibilities, and major recent accomplishments (in business terms).

7. Futures: Maps future directions, including likely new systems, products, and services. What is the strategic direction of the organization regarding technology? What business and technical factors are influencing that direction? What products or environments are going to be phased out, and why? What products or environments will be emphasized, and why?

8. Information Technology Planning: Describes the process by which IS works with clients to build technology planning into business plans.

9. For More Information . . .: A directory of tools, services, and other items of interest with contact names and phone numbers. Should be on the back cover for quick reference.

OUTSIDE PUBLICATIONS

Though internal publications are a valuable marketing asset, they can require significant effort to maintain. Coverage for IS activities in external publications can produce impact with much less effort. Appropriate publications include trade journals and related publications in the IS industry, business publications, and local media (newspapers, magazines, radio, and television). The IS trade journals are always on the lookout for success stories. There are few better ways to get clients excited about technology than to have them cited as leading-edge users in a technology-oriented publication. In most cases all that is required is a phone call to their editorial office with a brief explanation of the story to bring an enthusiastic editor running. Give your client the visibility; the more the story focuses on the client, the better the impact on IS's image as a problem-solving partner. If the story involves a first-rate business success in which technology was used to significantly improve competitive position or bottom-line results, or to solve a problem which threatened the business, it may be of interest to national business publications in your industry.

Local publications are often overlooked marketing outlets. Most local newspapers now feature a daily or weekly business section. Many have columns or sections focused on information technology. In addition, metropolitan areas often support a paper dedicated to the local business community. These publications are always on the lookout for newsworthy material, and a relationship with their editorial staff can be valuable. This kind of exposure improves the image of the organization in the community while at the same time providing recognition for the client group and IS.

One word of caution is appropriate regarding all these outlets. Make sure that you follow any internal procedures for clearing information for publication and that the client(s) covered in the story, their management, and any other critical parties are fully aware and involved. Having the CEO or the client unpleasantly surprised by a piece in the paper is not good marketing.

SPEAKING ENGAGEMENTS

Giving presentations for external groups is another marketing method for IS. National or local IS conferences are always looking for speakers on particular topic areas, including case studies of "how we did it at XYZ Corporation." To build partnership into this effort, include your client on the presenting team. Even more effective in positioning IS as a problem-solving partner is speaking at conferences focusing on your organization's industry, with the focus on a technology initiative's impact on the business and its ramifications across the industry.

Also valuable are speaking engagements for local groups—universities from which your organization recruits, local business groups, high schools, civic organizations. The subject may range from career opportunities in information systems to developments in technology to the impact of new technologies on current business practices. These are good opportunities for you to gain presentation experience while building a positive image of the IS function and the organization in the community.

USER GROUPS

Vendors of computer hardware and software know the marketing value of user groups. By setting up meetings, publishing newsletters, and maintaining communication about the product, user groups develop a strong peer-to-peer, network-building awareness of a product. Vendors also find that this network becomes a free education resource, helping the users of the product help each other with problems and communicating solutions to each other. The networks also become a prime source of marketing information for the vendor on how to improve their products and services.

You can use this technique for the users of any major computer system or tool. Your role is to supply the initial push to get the group or groups started, and then let them operate relatively autonomously. This means generating interest, scheduling the first meeting, electing officers, supplying speakers, bringing the coffee and donuts, and then fading into the background so that the group can talk frankly about their own problems. Encourage communication between the groups and IS, particularly where problems and proposed solutions are involved; however, that communication does not have to happen during the meetings themselves. Every so often—every 6 to 12 months depending on the group—user groups benefit from a revitalization. Here you can help by bringing in an outside speaker or vendor representative to discuss new features, approaches used elsewhere, or other issues of interest to the group.

INFORMATION TECHNOLOGY FAIR

One effective way to improve awareness of computing technology's contribution to organizational success is to organize an event that recognizes accomplishments in this area: an internal information technology fair, a combination conference and exhibition that emphasizes real business improvements through technology. The fair should not sell IS itself, or even the technologies IS supports, but the benefits IS is in business to promote. This should be reflected in the name chosen for the event: "Technology for Competitive Advantage," "The Information Technology Edge," or some similar title in keeping with IS's charter as a business partner is important to communicate the right message.

Table 18–1 illustrates the key participants for a successful fair, the roles they can play, and the benefits they can expect from participating.

You will probably need full senior management support due to the

TABLE 18–1
Key Participants in the Information Technology Fair

Player	Roles	Benefits
Senior manager	Sponsor Keynote speaker Reward giver	Concrete means of rewarding and promoting effective use of technology Perception as involved in organization Perception as supporting innovative use of technology
Key clients	Success stories Missionaries Demonstrators	Reward for superior performance Higher visibility Perception as linked to organization goals
IS management and staff	Organizers Enthusiasm-builders	High-visibility marketing to a broad audience
Vendors and suppliers	Demonstrators Information providers	Rare chance to promote products internally to large audience Chance to learn customer's culture
Organization	Audience Potential IS customers	Chance to learn about technology in a non-threatening setting Chance to share experience of rest of organization

allocation of funds, time, and space required to make the fair work. Just as important as funding, however, is senior management's visible support. The best evidence of this is their participation in the fair, which can include giving a keynote address, or presiding at awards for effective use of technology. Gain senior management support in the planning stage, through a carefully prepared proposal and presentation selling the fair's benefits to them and to the organization.

Involving Key Clients
The bulk of the fair should consist of presentations and demonstrations of effective applications of information technology. These demonstrations can be scheduled like sessions at a trade show or conference, perhaps three or four times over the course of a two-day fair, so that people can arrange their schedules to see those they are interested in. Ensure that a good cross-section of the organization—and the technology tools used—is represented. Use your marketing map (see Chapter 15) to identify likely candidates.

A professionally prepared program, distributed a week in advance of the fair, is the best advertisement. It convinces people that something of significance is going to happen. Include:

- An introduction by senior management.
- Schedules for all events.
- Descriptions of all demonstrations.
- An article describing the information technology tools used and how to get information on access, training, and use.

The technology fair presents an opportunity for IS staff to talk to a large number of potential clients and build recognition and familiarity throughout the organization. Discussions during the fair can generate information that can be used to focus additional marketing efforts.

APPENDIX

SUMMARY CHECKLIST

The following checklist gathers key points, step-by-step procedures, and issues to remember from the preceding chapters. It is designed to be used as a quick refresher, a quick topic index to help you identify which chapter a particular technique is covered in, and a touchstone for testing your IS consulting activities against the partnership model. The page numbers where each subject included in the checklist can be found are listed at the right side of the page.

RESPONSIBILITIES IN THE PROBLEM-SOLVING PARTNER RELATIONSHIP   19

1. Consultant acts as change agent.
2. Client acts as change manager.
3. Both drive the problem-solving process. Roles are negotiated.
4. Two-way communication is designed into the project.
5. The focus is on the business problem and the work relationship in addition to the technical problem.
6. The action plan is jointly designed. Both have critical pieces of the puzzle.
7. Both actively identify needed data and jointly analyze the implications.
8. Both teach and learn from the other.
9. The consultant is the expert in the problem-solving process and provides the framework for this process.

FIFTEEN CHARACTERISTICS OF THE
PROBLEM-SOLVING PARTNER 20-22

1. Working with clients in an equal partnership.
2. Seeing things from the client's perspective.
3. Focusing on the work relationship with the client.
4. Communicating in the client's own language.
5. Working to build client trust, confidence, and commitment.
6. Absorbing information and redefining it as solvable problems.
7. Keeping the focus on desired results.
8. Generating and presenting options for solution.
9. Mobilizing effective action once a problem is defined.
10. Working with (not around) tension and conflict.
11. Being concerned and committed without taking anything personally.
12. Minimizing long-term client dependence on IS.
13. Facilitating (not taking over) the client's job responsibilities.
14. Staying out of no-win situations.
15. Loading the deck for success by preselling and building commitment wherever necessary.

THE CONSULTING CYCLE

Initial Contact Rules 37-42

1. Profile the client.
2. Establish rapport with the client.
3. Let the client know you've got the picture—that you:
   a. Understand the problem's key elements.
   b. Are not underestimating its difficulty.
   c. Are taking it seriously.
   d. Are interested in solving it.
4. Provide a problem-solving framework.
5. Before moving on to contracting, ask yourself:
   a. Does the client feel comfortable with me?
   b. Is the atmosphere conducive to negotiation on project roles?
   c. Do I have a clear understanding of the basic business problem?
   d. Does the client feel comfortable with my understanding of the problem?

e. Do I have the information I need to realistically begin negotiations on project issues?

Contracting Rules   43–53

1. Three legs make a contract:
   a. Business problem.
   b. Technology solution.
   c. Consultant/client work relationship.
2. Contracting means mutual agreement on:
   a. Parameters/limits of the project.
   b. Client's desired results.
   c. Client/consultant roles.
   d. Deliverables and schedule.
   e. Consultant's needs.
   f. Procedures and ground rules.
3. Make deposits before you make withdrawals.
4. Negotiating strategy:
   a. Client requirements.
   b. Consultant offers.
   c. Consultant requirements.
   d. Client offers.
5. Test the agreement.
   a. Pay attention to the client's reactions as the negotiations proceed.
   b. Empathize, trying to see your proposals as the client would see them.
   c. Watch for body language that expresses concern or confusion, or conflicts with the client's words.
   d. Listen for signs of concern, confusion, anxiety, lack of trust or confidence in the client's tone of voice.
   e. Listen to your own intuition about how the client is feeling.
   f. Check the energy level of the discussion. When it drops, there are probably unexpressed concerns.
   g. Use open-ended, neutral questions to give the client an opportunity to express concerns.
   h. Check how eager your client is to move onto the next step.
   i. Watch how your client follows through on the first few commitments of resource or time to the project.
6. Maintain communication with your client.

Contracting Checklist   47

Before moving on to data collection, ask yourself the following questions:

1. Is there mutual agreement on the goals of the project effort?
2. How do these goals translate into solvable problems?
3. Are client and consultant roles clear for:
   a. Data collection?
   b. Analysis?
   c. Recommendations?
   d. Decision making?
   e. Implementation?
   f. Evaluation?
4. Is there provision for follow-up and evaluation so that both parties can learn from the project?
   a. What is the agreed-upon evaluation method?
   b. What are the evaluation criteria?
5. Are all parties to the contract involved in the contracting process? If not, what other parties should be included?
6. What agreement exists on sharing responsibility for the project?
7. Are the requests and promises made realistic?
8. What agreement exists that the client's desired results are really needed:
   a. In the client's organization?
   b. In the consultant's organization?
9. Is the contract freely entered by both parties without coercion or misgivings?
10. Does the contract allow for renegotiation and necessary change along the way?

DATA COLLECTION AND ANALYSIS RULES   55–60

Building Trust and Motivation during Data Collection

1. Show the client he or she is in capable hands.
2. Be direct and honest in communicating with the client.
3. Communicate your commitment to the client.
4. Communicate an agenda in advance.
5. Provide immediate client benefit.

Controlling Data Collection Meetings 61

1. Take facilitative control.
2. Base your control on the agenda.

Recommendations Rules 62–69

1. Link recommendations clearly to the client's problem.
2. Present solution options for client review.
3. Make sure the options are clear to the client.
4. Make the client comfortable enough with the technology to make an informed decision.
5. Objectively describe the pros and cons of the options.

Decision-Making Rules 69–70

1. Decision making is the client's stage.
2. Client options include "no" and "none of the above."
3. Test client comfort and commitment to the solution.

Development/Assistance/Training Rules 71–72

1. Maintain communication with your client.
2. Use training to build partnership.
3. Use the trainer as a feedback loop.

Implementation Rules 72–75

1. Implementation is the client's responsibility.
2. Build support for the solution.
3. Use the consulting cycle to lay the groundwork.
4. Keep the communication lines open.

Evaluation Rules 75–80

1. Define evaluation criteria in the contracting stage.
2. Encourage the client to take the lead in evaluating the solution.
3. Base the evaluation on business criteria.
4. Use the data collection and analysis stage to verify and refine evaluation criteria.

5. Help the client see the solution in broader organizational terms.
6. Evaluate the consulting effort.
7. Use evaluation data to make the business case for IS.

End or Extend Rule   80–81

1. Use the evaluation data to determine next steps.

THE PARTNER MAP   85–89

1. Problem-solving partner.
   a. Partner you work with directly.
   b. May represent a group or a higher level client.
   c. Decision maker, accountable for project success.
2. Information partners.
   a. Those you need information from.
      1. Usually not decision makers.
      2. Provide data on project or environment.
   b. Those you need to keep informed.
      1. Part of resource network.
      2. Usually not directly involved in project.
      3. Can have impact on project.
      4. Should not be surprised by project developments.
3. Lobbying partners.
   a. Can speak up for project at key junctions with key audiences.
   b. May be part of client or consultant organization.
   c. Usually need to be sold on benefits to them.
4. Sponsor partners.
   a. Influential, opinion shapers.
   b. Can open doors and free up resources.
   c. Have significant stake in successful implementation.
5. Affected groups.
   a. Jobs, procedures, interfaces will change as a result of project.
   b. Can impact project momentum if not supportive.
6. Roadblocks.
   a. Likely to resist or object to project.
   b. Can be individuals, groups, cultural forces.

INTERACTIVE LISTENING: THE H.E.A.R. MODEL   90–95

1. Hear.
   a. Make a mental commitment to listen.
   b. Eliminate internal/external noise.
   c. Periodically feed back what you have heard to test for accuracy.
2. Empathize.
   a. Work to understand and respect the client's point of view even if yours is different.
   b. Listen for feelings/ideas.
   c. Paraphrase the client's position to test for accuracy.
3. Analyze.
   a. Hold off on analysis until you have finished stage 2.
   b. Walk the client through your analytical framework to build a *shared* analysis.
   c. Ask for feedback on what fits and what doesn't.
4. Respond.
   a. Use your response to add value.
   b. Respond in language the client will understand.
   c. Connect your response to previous areas of mutual agreement.
   d. Be specific about needed actions.
   e. Ask the client to paraphrase your response and comment on it.

STRUCTURING CLIENT MEETINGS FOR SUCCESS   96–107

1. Prepare.
   a. Define your objectives.
   b. Prepare an agenda.
   c. Communicate the agenda in advance.
   d. Prepare key questions.
   e. Make sure the relevance of questions is obvious.
   f. Don't include questions that produce data you can't handle.
   g. Pay attention to time and setting.
2. Open.
   a. Reduce anxiety.
   b. Review objectives.
   c. Review agenda.
   d. Review roles.

3. Conduct.
   a. Make sure the meeting is productive.
   b. Turn information into solvable problems.
   c. Clarify project roles.
   d. Use interactive listening.
   e. Provide immediate benefit to the client.
4. Close.
   a. Review and summarize.
   b. Next steps.
   c. Action commitments.
   d. Analysis of meeting.
5. Follow-up.
   a. Work with the data as soon as possible.
   b. Communicate frequently with the client.

PREDICTING AND MANAGING
CLIENT RESISTANCE

Potential Sources of Resistance   **109–113**

1. Do the client and other affected groups see a need to change the status quo?
2. Do those who will be affected by the change have an opportunity to give significant input on the project, beginning in the planning stages?
3. Does the investment/payback ratio make good business sense to the client?
4. Do those affected (top, middle, and first-line management as well as individual contributors) understand the change process itself?
5. Are key people in the client organization *perceived* to be in support of the change?
6. What partnership relationship exists between the client organization and IS?
7. What level of respect does the client have for the individual IS consultant heading up the project and for other key IS personnel involved in the project?

8. How disruptive is the change perceived to be to ongoing work?
9. Is the change proceeding at the right pace?
10. Does the learning curve seem manageable in view of other tasks?
11. What fear of failure exists?
12. Have client concerns for information availability, integrity, and security been addressed?
13. Is good two-way communication with the client maintained throughout the project?

A Strategy for Managing Resistance   113–116

1. Develop a client profile.
2. Identify symptoms of client resistance.
3. Bring the resistive behavior to the client's attention in non-blaming, nonemotional terms.
4. Allow the client to respond.
5. Work in partnership to clarify the client's concerns and negotiate mutually agreeable solutions.

IS MARKETING: ALIGNING IS SERVICES
WITH CLIENT NEEDS

Goals of Marketing   137

1. Clarifying roles.
2. Building relationships.
3. Communicating benefits.
4. Targeting opportunities.

Don'ts of Marketing   138

1. Don't market technologies.
2. Don't market yourself personally.
3. Don't sweep past failures or shortfalls under the rug.
4. Don't push IS services on anyone.

The Action Funnel for Targeting
High-Payoff Opportunities   140–142

1. Where?—Identify the areas with the highest likelihood of using information technology to leverage business opportunities.
2. Who?—Identify the likely sponsors for information technology initiatives, the likely lobbying partners, the movers and shakers who
   will make successful problem-solving partners.
3. What?—Identify the key activities in the area and analyze your IS
   product/service mix for likely matches with this area's business
   needs.
4. How?—Determine how you can best get entry into this area.
5. When?—What timing is best for your entry?

A Simple Marketing Methodology   143–147

1. Develop an audience profile.
2. Develop a list of positive and resistive issues.
3. Develop a marketing strategy.

Successful IS Marketing Approaches   148–162

1. Mission statement.
2. Walk-in center.
3. Capabilities presentation.
4. Scheduled presentations.
5. Brown bag sessions.
6. Capabilities brochure.
7. Client handbook.
8. Computing environment guide.
9. Newsletter.
10. Outside publications.
11. Speaking engagements.
12. User groups.
13. Information technology fair.

THE PROBLEM-SOLVING PARTNER'S BOOKSHELF: SUGGESTED READINGS

Consulting Bookshelf

The following publications provide a variety of perspectives on the theory and practice of consulting and change management.

Argyris, Chris. *Strategy, Change, and Defensive Routines*. Boston: Pitman Publishing, 1985.

Argyris, Chris; Robert Putnam; and Diana McLain. *Action Science*. San Francisco: Jossey-Bass, 1985.

Argyris, Chris and Donald A. Schon. *Organizational Learning: A Theory of Action Perspective*. Reading, Mass.: Addison-Wesley Publishing, 1978.

Beckhard, Richard and Reuben T. Harris. *Organizational Transitions: Managing Complex Change*. Reading, Mass.: Addison-Wesley Publishing, 1977.

Beer, Michael. *Organizational Change and Development: A Systems View*. Santa Monica, Calif.: Goodyear Publishing, 1980.

Blake, R. R. and J. S. Mouton. *Consultation*. Reading, Mass.: Addison-Wesley Publishing, 1976.

Block, Peter. *Flawless Consulting*. San Diego, Calif.: University Associates, Inc., 1981.

Cullen, Bernard J.; George O. Klemp, Jr.; and Lawrence A. Rossini. *Competencies of Organizational Effectiveness Consultants in the U.S. Army* (Army Project number 2Q263731A79, Working Paper L&M TA81-1). Alexandria, Virg.: U.S. Army Research Institute for the Behavioral and Social Sciences, 1981.

Effective Organizational Consultation: An Overview. New York: Delta Consulting Group, 1980.

Greiner, Larry E. and Robert O. Metzger. *Consulting to Management*. Englewood Cliffs, N.J.: Prentice-Hall, 1983.

Henderson, Bruce. "The Consultant's Role." Boston Consulting Group Pamphlet, 1980.

Kanter, Rosabeth Moss. *The Change Masters*. New York: Simon & Schuster, 1983.

Kelly, Robert E. "Should You Have an Internal Consultant?" *Harvard Business Review*, November-December 1979, pp. 110–120.

Kolb, D. A. and A. L. Frohman. "An Organization Development Approach to Consulting." *Sloan Management Review*, 1970, pp. 55–65.

Kotter, John P. *Power and Influence: Beyond Formal Authority.* New York: Free Press, 1985.

Nadler, D. A. *Feedback and Organization Development.* Reading, Mass.: Addison-Wesley Publishing, 1977.

Porter, Michael E. *Competitive Strategy—Techniques for Analyzing Industries and Competition.* New York: Free Press, 1980.

Schein, Edgar H. *Process Consultation: Its Role in Organization Development.* Reading, Mass.: Addison-Wesley Publishing, 1969.

_____. *Process Consultation: Lessons for Managers and Consultants.* Reading, Mass.: Addison-Wesley Publishing, 1987.

Steele, Fritz, *Consulting for Organizational Change.* Amherst, Mass.: University of Massachusetts Press, 1975.

Tichy, Noel. *Managing Strategic Change.* New York: John Wiley & Sons, 1985.

Turner, Arthur N. "Consulting Is More Than Giving Advice." *Harvard Business Review*, September-October 1982, pp. 120–129.

Information Systems Bookshelf

The following publications provide a sampling of recent thinking regarding the role of information systems in changing the way organizations work.

Henderson, John C. and Michael E. Treacy. "Managing End-User Computing for Competitive Advantage." *Sloan Management Review*, Winter 1986, pp. 3–14.

Inmon, William H. *Managing End-User Computing in Information Organizations.* Homewood, Ill.: Dow Jones-Irwin, 1986.

McFarlan, F. Warren and James L. McKenney. *Corporate Information Systems Management: The Issues Facing Senior Executives.* Homewood, Ill.: Dow Jones-Irwin, 1983.

Meyer, N. Dean and Mary E. Boone. *The Information Edge.* New York: McGraw-Hill, 1987.

Parsons, Gregory L. "Information Technology: A New Competitive Weapon." *Sloan Management Review*, Fall 1983, pp. 3–14.

Porter, Michael E. and Victor E. Millar. "How Information Gives You Competitive Advantage." *Harvard Business Review*, July-August 1985, pp. 149–160.

Rockart, John F. *The Changing Role of the Information Systems Executive: A Critical Success Factors Perspective* (CISR WP #85, Sloan WP

#1297–82). Boston: Center for Information Systems Research, Sloan School of Management, Massachusetts Institute of Technology, 1982.

Rockart, John F. and Christine Bullen, eds. *The Rise of Managerial Computing*. Homewood, Ill.: Dow Jones-Irwin, 1986.

Rockart, John F. and David W. De Long. *Executive Support Systems*. Homewood, Ill.: Dow Jones-Irwin, 1988.

Synnott, William R. *The Information Weapon*. New York: Simon & Schuster, 1987.

Synnott, William R. and William H. Gruber. *Information Resource Management—Opportunities and Strategies for the 1980s*. New York: John Wiley & Sons, 1981.

INDEX